National Trust

Book of Afternoon Tea

National Trust
Book of
Afternoon
Tea

Laura Mason

National Trust

Published in 2018 by
National Trust Books
43 Great Ormond Street
London WC1N 3HZ
An imprint of Pavilion Books Company Ltd

ISBN: 9781911358206

A CIP catalogue record for this book is available
from the British Library.

25 24 23 22 21 20 19 18
10 9 8 7 6 5 4 3 2 1

Reproduction by Mission, Hong Kong
Printed by Toppan Leefung Printing Ltd, China

This book can be ordered direct from the publisher
at the website: www.pavilionbooks.com, or try
your local bookshop.

Contents

Taking Tea

The novelist Henry James, who lived at Lamb House in Rye, East Sussex, between 1897 and 1916, wrote 'there are few hours in life more agreeable than the hour devoted to the ceremony known as afternoon tea'. He did stipulate circumstances, which included an idyllic summer afternoon and a mellow country house.

The former inhabitants of many National Trust houses were keen on afternoon tea and many society hostesses agreed with him. Notable among these were Teresa, the wife of Thomas, the 8th Lord Berwick, at Attingham Park in Shropshire, and Mrs Greville at Polesden Lacey in Surrey. Mrs Greville was especially strict about timing. The meal was served at five o'clock, and guests had to be prompt. When Beverley Nichols stayed at the house, he wrote that 'Tea is at 5 o'clock … and not at 5 minutes past … which means the Spanish ambassador, who has gone for a walk … hastily retraces his steps, and the Chancellor of the Exchequer hurries down the great staircase, and that various gentlemen rise from their chaise-longues ….'

> Anna, Duchess of Bedford, found she suffered a 'sinking feeling' in the long, food-free hours between breakfast and dinner.

Members of the Royal Family were often among the guests, and a room in the house is still known as the Tea Room.

The 'at home' teas of leisured Victorian and Edwardian households were afternoon parties with varying degrees of formality. They featured thin bread and butter (the slices rolled, so as not to soil the kid gloves all ladies wore), little sandwiches, toast cut into fingers, and small cakes. Some houses offered heartier food, such as scones fresh from the oven, and bread to be cut and made into more substantial sandwiches, more appealing to masculine taste. These teas are the inspiration for many now offered in smart cafés and hotels throughout Britain, featuring delicate finger food: tiny sandwiches, pastries, fragile little cakes and biscuits, maybe with scones, or pieces cut from larger cakes, dainty and pretty, as if to say, this is not really a meal.

The history of afternoon tea is obscure; although a few morsels of light food were offered with a drink of tea in the eighteenth century, it is often dated to about 1840, when Anna Russell, Duchess of Bedford, found she suffered a 'sinking feeling' in the long, food-free hours between breakfast and dinner. The latter

had become an evening meal in fashionable life (lunch as it is now understood did not exist). Anna's solution to the problem was an afternoon drink of tea, accompanied by a little food. While visiting the Duke of Rutland at Belvoir Castle in Leicestershire, she invited her female friends to partake, and so originated afternoon tea, or 'five o'clock tea', as it is sometimes known.

Tea itself is a drink of Far Eastern origin. An expensive luxury when it first arrived from China in the seventeenth century, it became the height of fashion. In the eighteenth century, tea drinking gave opportunities to display fine porcelain teaware, and costly silver teapots. Many National Trust houses have examples of these. The Duchess of Lauderdale's teapot at Ham House in Surrey is a precious and unusual Chinese porcelain thought to have been owned by Elizabeth Murray, Countess of Dysart and later Countess and Duchess of Lauderdale (1626–1698). Ickworth near Bury St Edmunds, Suffolk, boasts a pair of spectacular George II teacaddies.

Tea gardens flourished at this time, their pleasant surroundings providing musical and other entertainments. Food, especially bread and butter, was offered alongside tea, but seems to have been secondary. The tax on tea was massively reduced in 1784 and tea drinking was taken up by all classes. The price of tea dropped again when the British established plantations in India and Ceylon in the mid-nineteenth century. Deep coloured, richly flavoured black teas taken with milk and sugar became the accustomed drink for many.

By the end of the nineteenth century, the idea of afternoon tea was firmly established. But, confusingly, 'tea' was also a name for another late afternoon meal, one for busy people who came home from work hungry, ate and then relaxed or went out again. These meals were associated with regional and rural households, and also with poorer people. This type of tea would have been eaten in the Birmingham Back to Backs, and in farmhouses such as Townend at Troutbeck in the Lake District. Ham was a favourite item, as were eggs and various types of fish, especially those preserved by smoke. Winter teas included a hot dish; summer ones might run to salads and cold meats. When adopted by the wealthy metropolitan elite as an informal evening meal, this became known as high tea, to differentiate it from afternoon tea. Invitations to tea were laden with social nuances: one might end up faced with far more food than expected, or possibly with rather less.

Afternoon tea came to mean different things to different people. Children in wealthy households had their nursery or schoolroom tea of boiled eggs, bread and butter and other plain food. Families relaxed around a tea table, as depicted in Sir Winston Churchill's painting *Tea at Chartwell, 29th August 1927*. In country houses, afternoon teas included heartier

> Cricket, too, is inextricably associated with tea – does any other sport routinely have a tea break?

food for guests who had spent the day in the open air: scones, buns, fruit cakes. There were teas for gatherings to play fashionable games such as croquet or lawn tennis; late-nineteenth century cooks even created a special oblong cake, iced and decorated to resemble a tennis court. Cricket, too, is inextricably associated with tea – does any other sport routinely have a tea break? And gentlemen's clubs offered savoury food for members in need of late afternoon sustenance.

Items appeared on the table as ordained by date or personal taste, for Christmas, Sundays, birthdays. Localities, too, were noted for certain things: cream teas in the south-west of England, griddle-baked cakes and breads in Wales, and a rich selection of home-baking, such as parkin, at tea tables in the north. Other foods evoked nostalgia: muffins, touted round foggy winter London streets by vendors who rang bells to announce their presence; or the 'honey still for tea', which Rupert Brooke wove into his poem *The Old Vicarage, Grantchester*, written in 1912.

A chance to dress up and socialise, or the centre of a busy family routine, a pause in a work-loaded day, an excuse for a chat, a biscuit or more, snatched in a break or taken at leisure, tea means many things to many people. It has become a constant in British culture, much enjoyed by all.

Different Types of Tea

Tea, the drink, is made from the dried leaves of *Camellia sinensis*, an evergreen shrub first cultivated in subtropical regions of China. Buddhism took the plant and drink to Japan. Silk Road caravans took tea, often compressed as bricks, to Central Asia and Russia. European trade brought China tea to the west and then spread cultivation to countries such as India, Sri Lanka and Kenya. This dynamic history, combined with the tastes of many different cultures, has given rise to many types of tea, differentiated by leaf size, processing, region and various other factors.

> This dynamic history, combined with the tastes of many different cultures, has given rise to many types of tea.

Processing is an important way of classifying teas, according to the level of oxidation (when the plucked leaves are exposed to the atmosphere for minutes or hours, withering and discolouring from green to black).

White teas are the least processed, produced from the shoots and top few leaves of the plant, which are simply dried. They are generally, but not invariably, low in caffeine and produce a drink that is pale in colour with a delicate taste and aroma.

Green teas are now considered a healthy choice in the range of teas, as processing – which involves a stage of heating to halt oxidation – inhibits the development of caffeine and preserves antioxidants, as well as the green colour. Matcha is a type of Japanese green tea, in which the leaves are ground and the powder mixed with water.

Oolong teas are partially oxidised and have more complex flavours than green teas; the best are beautifully fragrant. The leaves can be re-infused several times.

Black teas are by far the most commonly consumed teas in the UK. These are fully oxidised, giving a higher caffeine content and a range of coppery and chestnut brown colours and malty flavours familiar to British tea drinkers.

Tea is also graded according to leaf size, shape and the part of the plant it comes from, from whole leaf to dust; despite its unpromising name the latter can be sought after to produce dark, strong tea ideal for drinking with milk. It is also used in tea bags. Larger leaves are sometimes rolled into balls to give pearl teas or Gunpowder tea; the process aids flavour retention and makes for easier packing. Flower teas consist of hand-rolled and tied leaves, green or white, which unfurl in water to give a bloom-like effect. Orange Pekoe, despite its colloquial use as a name for various black teas, actually is a description of the grade of leaf rather than a blend.

Some areas produce single-estate teas; these are unblended and vary from year to year.

Blended teas are produced by mixing two or more tea varieties and include several British favourites. English Breakfast Tea is a blended black tea intended to be drunk with milk, a good accompaniment to sweet foods. Earl Grey is a mild-tasting black tea scented with bergamot oil, giving a citrus note. Lapsang Souchong has a distinctive pungent, smoky taste created by drying black tea leaves over pine-wood fires. Russian Caravan, another pungent black tea with a slightly smoky flavour and dark colour, originated from the tradition of carrying tea overland from China to Russia. Jasmine tea, typically a white or green tea, is scented by contact with fresh jasmine blossoms, which only release their fragrance at night.

Other drinks produced by steeping dried leaves or plant matter in hot water are technically known as infusions. One which has recently become popular in Britain is Rooibos, or Red Bush (*Aspalathus linearis*), of South African origin. The leaves are plucked, oxidised and dried to give a drink that is high in antioxidants and caffeine-free. Numerous other herbal infusions – sometimes referred to as herb teas – have long histories and are often marketed with claims for beneficial effects on health. Some of the most popular are chamomile (soothing), ginger, mint (both good for the digestion), liquorice (for respiratory problems), and many fruit, flower and spice blends enjoyed principally for flavour.

How to Make a Good Pot of Tea

Making a pot of tea is a comforting ritual embedded deep in British culture, and everyone knows how to do this – or do they? This is not about a tea bag in a mug of hot water (however quick and convenient this may be). Really good tea deserves attention and thought. The general instructions for making tea in the British way have remained more or less consistent since the mid-nineteenth century, and refer specifically to black teas such as Assam. Once you are equipped with a suitably sized teapot, this is how to go about it.

> Really good tea deserves attention and thought.

The water should be freshly drawn. Soft water is best. Those who are really serious about tea use filtered tap water or spring water. Fill the kettle and bring it to the boil. The tea should be made as soon as the water boils (if it is allowed to go on boiling, or re-boiled, the tea will taste flat), so the pot must be ready. Warm it, either by filling it with hot water and leaving it to stand for a few minutes before pouring the water away, or by swilling hot water round the pot and emptying it. Take the pot to the kettle.

Add the tea: the usual instruction is to add one teaspoonful of loose-leaf tea per person and one for the pot (omit the latter if not keen on very strong tea). Pour in the freshly boiled water from the kettle and leave to stand for 3–5 minutes if drinking it black, a minute or two longer if adding milk. Then pour through a strainer into cups. Hand sugar and thin lemon slices for black tea, or sugar and milk otherwise.

Tea which has been left to stand for a longer time on the leaves develops an unpleasantly bitter flavour. It is best to discard the used leaves and start again. Alternatively, use a pot with an infuser, so the leaves can be removed and further cups can be drunk at leisure. Tea bags (the most popular way of purchasing tea in Britain) act as disposable infusers and can easily be removed when the brew is the correct strength. Use a tea cosy to keep the pot warm.

Green or white teas have a slightly lower optimum water temperature of 80°C; for Oolong tea it is 80–90°C. For these teas, leave the water in the kettle to cool a little before pouring onto the tea leaves. These teas are drunk without milk. Oolong leaves can be removed, rinsed in cool water, and kept aside for re-infusion later in the day.

Rooibos, herbal and fruit infusions lack tannin; they should be brewed with boiling water and left to infuse for 4 minutes or longer, until they reach the desired strength of flavour. Milk is not added to these, except perhaps to Rooibos.

Apart from these pointers, tea making is largely down to individual taste and sense of occasion. The elegant paraphernalia of silver kettles, teapots, sugar boxes and creamers, porcelain tea services and finely crafted wooden caddies can be seen in almost any big house. For a formal occasion, you might like to emulate the historical precedents: use a pretty china tea set, line the serving dishes with dish papers or doilies and the tea tray with an embroidered cloth. For a more informal high tea, use an earthenware Brown Betty pot and a cheerful tea cosy. Although chunky ceramics are often used for serving tea, especially on casual occasions, it is nicer sipped from thin-walled containers, so china mugs are to be preferred over the heftier offerings.

There is one final question: to add milk to the cup before the tea or afterwards? Both sides claim logic: the 'milk in first' camp claim a longer precedent, saying that, originally, a little milk in the base of a precious porcelain tea bowl or cup helped lessen the possibility of it cracking when the hot tea was added. Proponents of adding milk after the tea say that hot tea scorches and cooks the milk very slightly, impairing the flavour, and also that adding milk later allows the drinker accurately to adjust the quantity according to taste. Perhaps it's best just to think that it is your cup of tea, and it should be how *you* like it.

> There is one final question: to add milk to the cup before the tea or afterwards?

Iced Tea

Perfect on a hot summer day, and a good alternative to alcohol-based punches, iced tea is a favourite drink in the USA, and deserves to be better known in Britain. (Note: this is not the same a Long Island Iced Tea, which is a powerful cocktail of various spirits.)

5 teaspoons black tea leaves: Darjeeling is a good choice, but Taylors China Rose Petal tea, a black tea blended with dried rose petals, is my favourite
2 teaspoons sugar, or to taste

Enough ice to fill 4 large tumblers
Thin strips of lemon zest

TO GARNISH (OPTIONAL)
Mint or borage sprigs, or fresh scented rose petals, or 1 white peach, skinned and thinly sliced

Put the tea leaves in a warmed pot or jug and pour over 500ml freshly boiled water. Leave to steep for 4 minutes, then strain the tea into a jug and discard the leaves. Stir the sugar into the tea until it dissolves; you may wish to use a little more.

Fill the tumblers with ice and divide the tea between them – the quantity of ice should be sufficient to chill and dilute the tea to a pleasing cold drink. Add a strip of lemon zest to each glass and garnish, if liked, with a sprig of mint or borage, a rose petal, or a slice of peach.

Moroccan Mint Tea

Refreshing in the Moroccan heat, and a good summer alternative to ordinary tea. If you can grow or buy Moroccan mint – *Mentha spicata crispa* var. 'Moroccan' – the tea will be even better. If you have Moroccan tea glasses use them; otherwise choose tall shot glasses, or fine porcelain cups.

3 tablespoons sugar, or to taste
3 teaspoons green tea, such as
  Gunpowder

A large handful of fresh spearmint,
  washed, plus a few sprigs to
  garnish (optional)

Warm a teapot or jug with boiling water. Set the kettle to boil. You will need about 1 litre water.

Drain any water from the warmed teapot and add the sugar, tea and mint. As soon as the kettle boils, fill up the pot with boiling water. Leave to stand for 3 minutes (no longer, or the tea will become bitter).

Pour the first glass of tea and immediately return this to the pot: this action helps ensure all sugar is dissolved.

Then pour a glass or cup of tea for everyone, raising the teapot high so that the stream of tea produces a light froth on the top of each glass (do this in the garden or over the draining board to avoid accidents to precious furnishings).

Add a sprig of mint to each glass if you wish. Sip, close your eyes and dream of Fez or Marrakech.

Masala Chai

Spiced tea, made in the style of India, is a soothing, uplifting drink for cold weather, good with toast or muffins. The spices can be varied to taste – star anise, coriander, saffron and almonds are found in recipes from various regions. I find an infinitesimal pinch of salt – just a few grains – improves the flavour.

6 whole cloves
6 cardamom pods
1 cinnamon stick
½ teaspoon black peppercorns
2cm cube of fresh ginger, peeled
    and cut into 3 or 4 slices

1 litre water
200ml milk
3 tablespoons sugar, or
    to taste
6 teaspoons black tea,
    such as Assam

Put all the spices and the water in a saucepan and bring to the boil. Cover, turn off the heat, and leave to infuse for 5–10 minutes.

Add the milk and sugar and return to the boil. Add the tea leaves and remove from the heat once again. Leave to infuse for a further 2–3 minutes, then strain into a teapot or into cups and serve immediately.

Bread and Butter and...

Cucumber and Minted Cream Cheese Sandwiches

Cucumber is the classic choice for elegant traditional teas.

200g cream cheese
Leaves from 4–5 sprigs of
  mint, chopped coarsely

6–8 thin slices of bread from
  a white tin loaf
½ peeled cucumber, thinly sliced

Mix the cream cheese and mint and divide among the slices of bread, spreading it carefully almost to the crust. Layer the cucumber over half the slices. Top with the remaining bread, trim the crusts and cut into triangles or fingers.

Tomato and Basil Sandwiches

A lovely summery combination. The National Trust's Wimpole Estate in Cambridgeshire hosts an annual tomato festival, displaying many varieties of this vibrant fruit.

1 large beef tomato
6–8 thin slices of bread from
  a white tin loaf
Softened butter

Salt and black pepper
Leaves from 2 or 3 sprigs
  of fresh basil, torn
3–4 tablespoons mayonnaise

Remove the core of the tomato, where the stem was, by cutting it out in a small conical plug. Slice the tomato across very thinly.

Spread half the slices of bread with a little softened butter. Distribute the tomato slices over these. Sprinkle with salt and pepper, and scatter with pieces of basil leaf.

Spread the remaining bread slices with the mayonnaise and use them to cover the tomatoes. Press lightly together and trim the crusts. Cut each sandwich crossways into three fingers, and then make a single cut lengthways to give six small square pieces per round.

At Home Tea

'At home' teas originated as tea parties, so naturally, tea is the focus. With it, offer milk or lemon and a bowl of lump sugar, though as Henry Fielding wrote in the eighteenth century: 'love and scandal are the best sweeteners of tea'. Coffee and alcoholic drinks may also be offered, remembering that a glass of good dry white or red wine is better with afternoon tea treats than sweet wines; sherry or Madeira are alternatives. Especially festive and celebratory teas might include sparkling wine or a drink based on this (pages 152 and 153), an English classic such as Pimm's (page 155) or perhaps a tea cocktail (page 154). Iced tea (page 17) or mint tea (page 18) are both excellent choices on a hot summer day.

> Henry Fielding wrote in the eighteenth century: 'love and scandal are the best sweeteners of tea'.

Use pretty china, present the food on nice plates or cake stands and try to find some exquisite linen cloths for trays or the table on which the food is set out. Seating should be comfortable and informal, with little tables on which to put cups and plates. Set parameters for time – say three till five o'clock, or four o'clock till six – and within this guests may come and go at times to suit themselves.

Such teas are not intended to be filling, so keep the food dainty. Any tiny sandwiches (this chapter includes some classic ideas) are appropriate, as are savoury profiteroles (page 108), gougères (page 110), little quiches (page 111) or savoury tartlets (page 112), and blinis with smoked salmon (page 128). Toast with anchovy butter (page 39) or cinnamon toast (page 38), are welcome in winter. Add a choice of two or three small cakes or pastries from Chapters 4 and 5; meringues are particularly good with summer berries. But remember that the elaborate 'at home' teas of the nineteenth century depended on a large kitchen staff, and don't overdo the choices. Better to do a few things well, rather than divide attention between many.

'At home' teas were heavily skewed towards late nineteenth-century feminine tastes. Men had their own equivalents in tea at the club: savoury food such as cheese on toast (page 40), Scotch woodcock (page 41) and club sandwiches (page 33). Scones (page 124) with jam and cream or savoury scones (page 125) are appropriate additions for those with heartier appetites.

Smoked Salmon Pinwheel Sandwiches

This idea came from food writer Bee Wilson, though I have tweaked the seasoning and the method a little.

1 small wholemeal tin loaf,
   freshly baked
200–250g cream cheese
Finely chopped fresh dill

Black pepper
Lemon juice
200–250g smoked salmon,
   thinly sliced

Chill the loaf for a couple of hours. Then take a bread knife, dip it in a jug of hot water and dry it before cutting a thin slice from the loaf at right angles to the base. Repeat until you have six thin slices (there will be some left over), dipping the knife in hot water and drying it between each slice. The dipping process makes it easier to cut neat slices.

Pass a rolling pin back and forth across each slice of bread to flatten it a little. Spread a thin layer of cream cheese on each slice. Season each with a little chopped dill, some black pepper and a few drops of lemon juice. Distribute the slices of smoked salmon neatly and evenly over the top.

Trim the crusts. Take each slice, make an indent with the back of a table knife on one short end and roll carefully and tightly to the other end. Wrap tightly in clingfilm and chill well.

Just before serving, discard the wrappings and use a sharp knife to slice each roll crossways to give four or five little pinwheels.

Egg and Cress Sandwiches

Egg sandwiches are a favourite with many people. Although not traditional, a tiny drop of chilli sauce perks up the flavour.

6 hard-boiled eggs, peeled and
   chopped into large chunks
1–2 tablespoons English mustard
3–4 tablespoons mayonnaise
Salt and pepper to taste

Chilli sauce, such as Tabasco
   or piri-piri sauce (optional)
Butter
16–18 small bread rolls
A punnet of mustard cress

Mix the eggs, mustard and mayonnaise, seasoning to taste with salt and pepper. If using Tabasco or piri-piri sauce, add just a couple of drops, stir well and taste. There should be just enough to give a hint of a bite and no more.

Butter the rolls and use the mixture to fill, garnishing each with a pinch of mustard cress.

Chicken and Curried Mayonnaise Sandwiches

For the chicken, leftovers from a roast can be used, but it is nice to cook the meat especially: poach a couple of large chicken breasts in water with a bay leaf, a few peppercorns, a piece of onion and ½ teaspoon of salt for about 15 minutes. Leave to cool.

Sunflower oil for frying
1 small onion, peeled and
   very finely chopped
2–4 teaspoons Madras
   curry powder
4 dried apricots, chopped small
A generous tablespoon mango
   chutney (chop any large pieces)

150g mayonnaise
200g cooked chicken
Salt
30–40g flaked almonds, toasted
16–18 small bread rolls
Roughly chopped coriander leaves
   or thinly sliced spring onions
   to garnish

Heat a little oil in a frying pan and cook the onion gently to soften it (don't let it brown). Stir in the curry powder and continue to cook gently for a few minutes. Remove from the heat and mix in the apricots and chutney. Leave to cool, then mix with the mayonnaise.

Cut the chicken into 1cm dice. Mix into the curried mayonnaise, taste, and add a little salt if necessary. Stir in the almonds.

Divide the mixture among the rolls, adding a little chopped coriander or a couple of very thin slices of spring onion to each.

These can be made a couple of hours in advance. Chill until needed.

Asparagus Rolls

Afternoon tea sandwiches are generally not served warm, but it is worth making an exception for these delicious morsels. If necessary, prepare them in the morning and then heat just before serving.

200g fresh asparagus spears
180g full-fat cream cheese
9 thin rashers of bacon or
  pancetta, cooked until crisp
About 2 tablespoons finely
  chopped chives

9 thin slices of white bread
About 50g butter, melted
30–40g Parmesan cheese,
  very finely grated

Preheat the oven to 200°C. Lightly grease a baking tray.

Cook the asparagus in salted boiling water until tender but not overcooked (you want a little 'bite' left). Drain, rinse well with cold water, then set aside to drain. Work the cream cheese to soften it, then crumble in the bacon and stir in the chives.

Roll each slice of bread with a rolling pin to flatten it, then trim off the crusts. Divide the cream cheese mixture among the slices of bread, spreading it right to the edges. Place an asparagus spear at the short end of each slice and roll up firmly. Brush the rolls lightly with melted butter, then roll them in the grated Parmesan. Place each one seam side down on the baking tray.

Bake for about 10 minutes until the outside is golden and crisp. Cut each roll in half crossways and serve while still warm and crunchy.

Banana and Clotted Cream Sandwiches

A special sandwich for a child's party, or a sweet treat for anyone, these are based on the Devon notion of 'thunder and lightning' – honey or golden syrup combined with clotted cream. Use crème fraîche for a slightly less calorific version.

3 bananas
½ a lemon
A small brown tin loaf,
  or a walnut loaf

About 75g clotted cream,
  or more to taste
2–3 tablespoons runny
  honey or golden syrup

Peel the bananas and slice thinly into a shallow bowl. Squeeze over the lemon and toss the slices to coat them in the juice.

Slice the bread thinly to give 6–8 slices. Spread half the slices with clotted cream and distribute the sliced banana over these. Spread the remaining slices with honey or golden syrup and use these to cover the cream and banana. Press down lightly to help the sandwiches hold together.

Cut each sandwich into quarters. Leave the crusts on, especially if using walnut bread: these are not intended to be especially dainty.

Sandwiches à l'Impériale

To really find out what can really be done with a sandwich, turn to Mrs Agnes Marshall, a late nineteenth-century cookery writer noted for elaborate food. These sandwiches – which she considered suitable for 'a savoury for dinner or luncheon, or as a breakfast dish, or for any cold collation' – show how commercial bloater paste, a popular nineteenth-century item made from a humble cured fish, might be turned into a work of art. The finishing touch – coral – is possibly Mrs Marshall's red-coloured, pepper-based garnish.

'*Cut some fresh brown bread in slices about quarter of an inch thick, and then mask it with the following mixture: Take for eight or ten persons two ounces of Gibson's cream of bloater and three hard boiled yolks of eggs and pound them together; add a quarter of a pound of fresh butter, and work in the mortar until smooth; then rub through a hair sieve and mix into it by degrees a half gill of stiffly whipped cream; spread this on the bread, and sprinkle it all over with very finely shredded celery that has been kept in cold water for about an hour to get crisp, then strain from the water and season with a little salad oil, chopped tarragon and chervil, a very little French vinegar, and a tiny dust of salt; close the cream in by placing another slice of bread on the top; butter this and sprinkle with the hard boiled yolk of an a egg that has been passed through a sieve, and over this, lightly sprinkle with chopped parsley, cut out the bread in strips, and with the mixture prepared as above make a little rose on the top of each sandwich with a rose pipe and bag; dish up on a dish-paper and garnish with green parsley and coral.*'

Club Sandwiches

Club sandwiches probably developed in North America in the late nineteenth century; they soon crossed the Atlantic and were a welcome and satisfying savoury bite for larger appetites.

6 thin slices of white bread
Mayonnaise
About 150g cooked chicken or
    turkey breast, thinly sliced
Salt and pepper

4–6 crisp lettuce leaves
Softened butter
4 rashers of good-quality
    back bacon, grilled
2 tomatoes, thinly sliced

Toast the bread lightly. Put two slices on a board and spread with a thin layer of mayonnaise: enough to coat the bread but not so much it squeezes out of the sandwich. Cover with the slices of chicken or turkey, season with salt and pepper and top with a good layer of lettuce leaves.

Thinly butter the next two slices of toast, and place them, butter side down, over the lettuce. Spread another layer of mayonnaise across their upper surfaces. Divide the bacon between the two sandwiches. Cover with sliced tomato.

Butter the remaining two slices of toast and put them butter side down over the bacon and tomato. Press together lightly. Cut in half diagonally, and again, to give four little sandwiches per round. Use a cocktail stick to secure each sandwich, and serve immediately.

For High Tea

Toast

Toast has long been a feature of tea at home. For nursery teas and farmhouse teas it was made before the fire, the bread speared on a toasting fork. On formal occasions it was made in the kitchen; here are instructions for Buttered Toast from Miss M.L. Allen, from her book *Five O'Clock Tea* (1887). Her ingredients list is simple and unspecific:

1 tin loaf
Salted butter

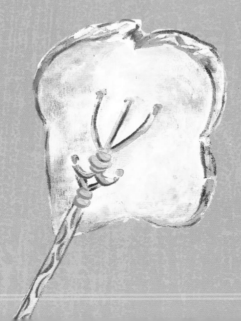

Cut your slices of bread half an inch thick and toast on both sides before a clear fire.

Put in a plate, butter thickly and cut the crusts off each slice.

The toast should be put in the oven a few minutes before being served, and sent to table in a hot muffin dish. The pieces of toast should be no larger than 2½ inches square.

Note:
'A delicate, thin square of toast spread with fresh dripping is by no means to be despised, and indeed is extensively ordered by doctors for persons suffering from dyspepsia and other disorders. A little salt sprinkled over the dripping is a great improvement.'

Melba Toast

Miss Allen didn't suggest Melba toast, which is an excellent accompaniment to potted meats and pâtés.

Cut thin slices from an ordinary white tin loaf and toast. Then trim off the crusts and carefully use a serrated knife to slice through the crumb between the toasted sides. Cut each piece in half diagonally. Put the bread, toasted side down, under a moderate grill until the inner side is lightly toasted. It will brown in pleasingly uneven patches but burns easily, so watch it carefully.

Cinnamon Toast

On its own, or as part of a larger spread – afternoon or high tea – this is brilliant with a cup of your favourite brew on a raw winter's day. These quantities are about right for 6 slices of toast. The sugar and spice mixture can be made in advance, in larger quantities if desired, and stored in a jar.

2 tablespoons caster sugar
Seeds from 4–5 cardamom pods,
   finely ground

1 scant teaspoon ground cinnamon
Bread for toast
Butter

Mix the sugar and spices.

White bread cut from a decent quality tin loaf is best. Cut it fairly thin, toast and then butter immediately. Dredge with the spiced sugar so that it combines with the melted butter. If feeling posh, trim the crusts and cut the toast into fingers.

Anchovy Butter

Anchovy butter is excellent on toast and in Scotch woodcock (page 41) and also goes well in sandwiches with a little crisp salad such as thin slices of radish or iceberg lettuce.

40g anchovy fillets, drained of oil
200g butter, softened
Pinch of cayenne pepper

Small pinch of ground
roasted cumin (optional
– see note)

Put all the ingredients in a blender and whizz to an even paste.
Scrape into a bowl and chill until needed.

This can be made ahead, divided into smaller portions and frozen.

Note:
To make the roasted cumin: toast whole cumin seeds for a few
minutes in a dry frying pan until they release their aroma, and
then grind in a spice grinder. Store in an airtight jar.

Cheese on Toast

There are many versions of cheese on toast and rarebits. This is mine: it is a method rather than a recipe, so increase the quantities to suit.

1 or 2 slices of bread: use brown or white tin loaf, or bloomer as preferred. Sourdough is an option, but the crusts can harden during toasting.
Butter (optional)
½–1 tablespoon of your favourite chutney: I prefer a tomato chutney with a good amount of chilli and a savoury undernote, but a sweeter, milder one works equally well. Chop any large pieces of fruit or vegetable in it before use.
30–60g good-quality cheddar, very thinly sliced

Toast one side of the bread under the grill. Remove it and turn the toasted side down on a baking tray. Spread the untoasted side with a little butter if desired. Then spread with chutney, taking this right to the edges of the crusts. Distribute the cheese over the top, breaking the slices to fit. Again, they should reach the edge of the bread. If the slices of bread are large, you may need more cheese.

Put the cheese-covered bread back under the grill and cook until the cheese has melted and is starting to bubble.

The slices can be cut into smaller pieces and eaten from the fingers. Be careful, as the chutney is very hot when this has come directly from the grill.

Serves 1

Scotch Woodcock

**A classic Victorian savoury, this makes a good hot dish
for tea – but is strictly for those who like anchovies.**

1 slice of white bread
Anchovy butter (page 39)
2 eggs

Salt and pepper
About 10g unsalted butter
2 anchovy fillets, drained of oil

Toast the bread, spread with anchovy butter, place on a heated
serving plate and keep warm.

Break the eggs into a bowl and season with a small pinch of salt
and a generous grind of black pepper. Beat together. Melt the butter
in a small pan (non-stick for preference) and add the egg mixture.
Stir over moderate heat to scramble the eggs – they should be a
soft-textured mass. When they are done, pour them over the hot
toast. Place the two anchovy fillets in a cross over the top and serve
immediately.

Note:
If the cook has failed to make anchovy butter, then plain butter and
a little Patum Peperium (Gentleman's Relish, essentially an anchovy
paste) can be used instead, or plain butter, though these options make
for less harmonious flavours.

Little Cheese Puddings

**Cheese and eggs were standbys in farmhouse kitchens.
This is based on a Welsh recipe for using them.**

6 thin slices white bread,
   crusts removed
Butter, for spreading and greasing
120g Cheddar cheese, grated
180ml single cream

½ teaspoon dry mustard
Pepper
A pinch of cayenne
5 eggs, beaten
Watercress, to serve

Toast the bread on one side. Butter the untoasted side. Butter
6 individual ovenproof ramekins and line each ramekin with
a slice of the bread, toasted side down. Divide the cheese
between the dishes.

Bring the cream to the boil, add the mustard and spices
and beat in the eggs. Pour over the bread and cheese.

Rest for 30 minutes, then bake at 190°C for 20–25 minutes,
until well-risen and light brown. Serve immediately with
a salad of watercress or bitter leaves, such as rocket.

Smoked Trout Pâté

Afternoon teas and high teas often featured fish pastes. This is a modern equivalent. Smoked mackerel or hot-smoked salmon can be used instead.

About 150g hot-smoked trout
80g cream cheese
20g butter, melted and cooled
Finely grated zest of ½ a lemon
    and 1 tablespoon lemon juice
Large pinch of ground nutmeg
Black pepper
Salt (optional)

TO SERVE
Melba toast (page 37)
Chopped chives
Capers preserved in salt,
    rinsed

Flake the fish, removing any bones and skin. Mix with the cream cheese, melted butter, lemon zest and juice, and the nutmeg. Grind in some black pepper and taste. Add salt only if it seems necessary (the fish is already quite salty). Chill well.

This is best made a day in advance and will keep, chilled, for 2–3 days.

To serve, pack in a pretty dish, or use 2 teaspoons to shape into little quenelles on pieces of Melba toast. Garnish with chopped chives and a scatter of capers.

Potted Shrimps

Delicious with toast, or with wholemeal or sourdough bread. Shrimps make the best-flavoured version, but prawns are easier to buy.

About 150g poached white fish (cod, haddock, ling, whiting), cooled and free from skin and bones
About 100g cooked, shelled shrimps or prawns
Pinch of ground mace
Pinch of cayenne pepper
100g butter, plus about 50g for clarifying
1 small anchovy fillet, mashed, or ½ teaspoon nam pla (Asian fish sauce)
Salt

Put the fish in a food processor or blender. Add about half the shellfish, the mace, cayenne pepper, 100g butter cut in small cubes and the mashed anchovy fillet or the fish sauce. Whizz to a paste, being careful not to over-work.

Scrape into a bowl, taste and add more seasoning if necessary. Mix in the remaining shrimps or prawns (cut the latter into smaller pieces). Pack into a small china pot.

Gently melt the remaining 50g butter and strain it through muslin or kitchen paper. When it is cool but not set, pour in a layer over the top of the mixture. Keep chilled and eat within 24 hours.

High Tea and Farmhouse Teas

High tea is altogether a different proposition to afternoon tea. Taken at the dining-room (or in smaller houses, kitchen) table, featuring proper, filling food, this is a full evening meal eaten between five and six pm. Its name and origins are even more obscure than afternoon tea. To many people this was simply 'tea', the meal they ate when the day's work was done. The wealthy metropolitan elite seem to have adopted this meal as an occasional alternative to dinner. This also meant they needed a name to differentiate it from afternoon tea. But why high tea? 'High' may originally have meant the presence of a savoury course of meat or other 'proper' food. Alternatively, it might refer to the high dining table (as opposed to the low scatter tables used for afternoon tea); in *Shirley*, Charlotte Brontë describes an elaborate tea of bread and butter, preserves, ham, cheesecakes and tarts taken round a table, 'knees duly introduced under the mahogany'.

The teapot is ever-present in such a routine, filled with a brew of richly coloured Indian tea. Bread and butter accompanied substantial food: this chapter includes some suggestions, or make sausage rolls (pages 104 and 106) or a quiche or tart (pages 111 and 112). Alternatively, provide a plate of sliced cold meat, some salad and a choice of cheeses. Pickles for cold meat, and jam or honey to spread on the bread can also be added. The food historian Alan Davidson described how, in his childhood, a procession of scones, pancakes, biscuits, and cakes small and large followed the savoury food, with the richest cake eaten last of all.

Teas of this type have a long association with regional, rural and farmhouse food. Home baking was always important. Any farmer's wife worth her salt baked bread at home and kept the cake tins full.

A selection of shortbread, biscuits, small cakes and tarts, a fruit loaf, or at least one large cake were essential to the meal. Fancier items such as meringues (page 100) and éclairs (page 114) are not out of place at such teas, particularly on special days.

Ham and egg teas (page 50) were often provided by rural housewives and village inns as food for those pursuing the fashion for rambling in the 1920s and 30s. Similar meals – a fry-up of bacon or sausage and eggs with chips, followed by a cake stand, all washed down with tea – survived as a form of high tea in Scotland until recently.

Ham Salad

In *Barnaby Rudge* (1841), Charles Dickens describes a tea with ham
'garnished with cool green lettuce-leaves and fragrant cucumber'. If
the salad vegetables come fresh from the garden, so much the better.

2 small soft-leaved butterhead
  lettuces, broken into separate
  leaves and washed
½ a cucumber, or a small ridge
  cucumber, peeled and sliced
4–6 tomatoes, sliced
Radishes, washed and trimmed
4 nice slices of ham
English sauce for salad
  (see opposite)

OPTIONAL EXTRAS
Spring onions, washed and
  trimmed
A few small new potatoes, scraped
  and boiled in water with mint
A few fresh peas, briefly boiled
  with mint
Beetroot, boiled or baked
4 cold, hard-boiled eggs
Salmon, poached and cooled

Starting with the lettuce, arrange all the salad ingredients
(but not the sauce) in a suitable bowl.

Potatoes and peas should be freshly cooked but left to cool before
adding to the salad. Beetroot is better handled separately, as it will
colour anything it touches.

Hard-boiled eggs can be added as well, or substituted for the ham;
cold poached salmon can be used as well as or instead of the ham.

Serve the sauce in a jug.

English Sauce for Salad Meat or Cold Fish

A recipe adapted from Eliza Acton's book *Modern Cookery for Private Families* (1845), an alternative to mayonnaise or French dressing.

Yolks of 2 cold hard-boiled eggs (discard the whites, or chop and use to decorate the salad)
½ teaspoon salt
½ teaspoon sugar
Pinch of cayenne pepper
½ teaspoon English mustard

1 small clove of garlic, peeled and roughly chopped (optional)
1 small anchovy fillet (optional)
1–2 tablespoons wine vinegar or tarragon vinegar
150ml thick double cream or crème fraîche

Put everything except the cream in a blender and whizz together to make a paste. Scrape into a bowl. Stir in the cream. Taste and adjust the seasoning with more salt or vinegar if desired. Chill for a couple of hours before use.

Ham and Eggs

Ham and eggs can be simply fried eggs served with sliced cooked ham. Here, I've added a cream sauce, based on North American milk gravy – which is actually a roux-type sauce.

About 50g butter
2 gammon slices or steaks
2 teaspoons flour
About 150ml stock, cider or water

150ml single cream
Salt and pepper
2 eggs, or more if desired

Melt about a third of the butter in a large frying pan and fry the gammon gently for 5–7 minutes on each side. When done, remove the meat to a plate and keep warm.

Using a wooden spoon, stir the flour into the residue in the pan and cook for a moment. Add the stock, cider or water to the pan, stirring well to make a smooth sauce and incorporating all the residue from cooking the gammon. Cook until the liquid has reduced to a couple of tablespoons. Stir in the cream and bring to the boil. Taste to check the seasoning, adding salt or pepper as necessary, then pour into a warmed jug or small bowl.

Quickly clean the pan, return it to the heat, melt the rest of the butter, and fry the eggs. Divide them, the gammon and the sauce between two warmed plates and serve immediately.

Makes about
500g

Chicken Liver Pâté

A rich pâté of a type recalling Edwardian food. The standing mortar
in the kitchen at Castle Drogo in Devon would have been used for
smooth meat pastes of this type – a blender or food processor makes
the job much simpler.

400g chicken livers	150ml gin
125g butter	A scrap of orange zest,
2 shallots, peeled and	chopped (optional)
finely chopped	150ml double cream
1 generous teaspoon fresh thyme	1 teaspoon salt
leaves, roughly chopped	Black pepper

Check that any greenish parts have been removed from the livers and
cut into 1.5cm chunks. Melt a quarter of the butter in a large frying
pan and add the livers. Cook over moderate heat, stirring all the time,
until they are brown on the outside but still a little pink in the middle.
Use a slotted spoon to remove them to a food processor or blender.

Add the shallots and thyme to the pan and cook gently to soften, then
pour in the gin, add the orange zest, if using, and cook over high heat
until the liquid has reduced to about 3 tablespoons. Add to the livers
along with the cream, salt, pepper, and the remaining butter. Process
to a paste and rub through a sieve to ensure it is perfectly smooth.

Pack in a straight-sided dish and leave to cool. If desired, melt a little
extra butter and pour to form a layer over the top of the mixture.
Serve with toast for a special high tea, or use for sandwiches, or
as a filling for savoury profiteroles (page 108).

Herrings in Oatmeal

Plentiful and inexpensive, herrings were often eaten for high tea by those who couldn't afford to serve costly meat every day. This is one of the best ways of cooking them.

½ teaspoon salt
2 tablespoons fine oatmeal

2 fresh herrings, cleaned
 and filleted
Butter for frying

Mix the salt and oatmeal, and dip the herrings in it to coat them inside and out. Melt the butter in a large frying pan and fry the fish over low heat for 3–5 minutes on each side, depending on size. The coating should become brown and crisp. Serve immediately, with strong tea and bread and butter.

Jugged Kippers

When visiting Lindisfarne or Dunstanburgh Castle on the Northumberland coast, don't forget to buy kippers in Craster. These cold-smoked herrings made a high tea for many working families.

2 kippers
Butter, to serve

You will need a jug that is big enough to hold the kippers, so only the tips of the tails appear at the top of the jug. If you don't have a jug deep enough, the heads and tails can be cut off to shorten the fish.

Pour some boiling water in the jug to warm it, then pour it out. Put the kippers in the jug, heads down. Fill up the jug with boiling water, cover with a plate and leave for 5–7 minutes, depending on the size of the kippers.

Drain off the water and serve the fish on hot plates with a pat of butter on each.

If preferred, the kippers can be baked (with a pat of butter) in the oven at 190°C for 8–10 minutes.

Smoked Haddock and Leek Sauce

Smoked haddock, baked in milk with a poached egg on top, was a teatime treat. If you like, feel free to add one poached egg per person for a really substantial dish.

400g–450g smoked haddock
300–400ml milk
2 leeks, washed and trimmed
30g butter

20g flour
Salt and pepper
Chopped chives or parsley
Poached eggs (optional)

Preheat the oven to 220°C.

Put the haddock in an ovenproof dish and pour over the milk. Cover with a lid or foil and bake for 20 minutes or until the fish is done.

Meanwhile, slice the leeks finely (discard the greenest end of the leaves). Melt the butter in a heavy frying pan and sweat the leeks gently until soft.

Once the fish is cooked, remove it to a plate and keep warm. Stir the flour into the leek mixture, then add about two-thirds of the milk the fish was cooked in. Cook over moderate heat, stirring constantly until the mixture thickens to a sauce. Add a little more milk if it seems very thick. Taste and adjust the seasoning.

Serve the fish and sauce on warmed plates and scatter with chopped chives or parsley. If you are serving poached eggs as well, pop one on top of each fish.

Large Cakes

Whisked Sponge Cake

A feather-light alternative to richer cakes. The unusual method comes from a 1960s book called *Talking About Cakes* (a great subject for teatime) by Margaret Bates.

A little melted butter for greasing
4 large eggs, separated
Pinch of salt
120g caster sugar, plus
  a little for the tins

Finely grated zest of ½ lemon
120g plain flour, sifted, plus
  a little for the tins
Icing sugar, for dusting

Preheat the oven to 180°C. Prepare a ring mould or 2 x 20cm diameter tins: brush the inside with melted butter, then dust with a mixture of sugar and flour. You may wish to line the tin because the mixture tends to stick. Tap out any excess.

Put the egg whites in a large bowl, add a pinch of salt and beat with an electric whisk until stiff. Beat in a quarter of the caster sugar, then an egg yolk, and repeat until all are used, beating well between each addition. Add the lemon zest and continue beating until very light and thick (a trail should show behind the whisk).

Add the flour through a sieve, folding in swiftly and lightly with a metal spoon.

Scrape the mixture into the prepared mould or tins and bake for 20–25 minutes. The cake is done if it springs back when touched and is pulling away from the mould or tin a little. Cool in the tin for a few minutes, then turn out, placing it base down on a wire rack to prevent the top getting marked.

Arrange one of the cakes on a serving plate and spread with your choice of filling (this cake is particularly lovely with summer fruit, lemon curd, and whipped cream or crème fraîche). Top with the second cake. To serve, dust with icing sugar and cut into thin slices.

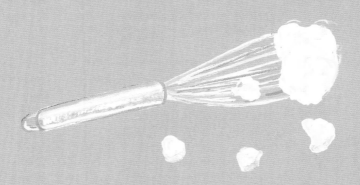

Victoria Sponge Cake

In 1861 Mrs Beeton gave a recipe for 'Victoria sandwiches', cake sandwiched with jam and cut into bars. They have become a British favourite, and the National Trust now serves its own version, below, in its tearooms around the UK.

175g caster sugar, plus
   extra to decorate
175g soft margarine
3 eggs, beaten
175g self-raising flour

4 tablespoons seedless
   raspberry jam
A punnet of fresh
   strawberries (optional),
   cut in quarters

Preheat the oven to 180°C. Grease 2 x 20cm Victoria sandwich tins and line the bases with non-stick baking paper.

Add the sugar and margarine to the bowl of your electric mixer and cream together until light and fluffy.

Gradually beat in the eggs little by little and beat well after each addition. If the mixture looks as if it may curdle, the addition of a little flour will bring it back.

Sift the flour over the cake mixture and gently fold in until smooth. Divide equally between the two tins and spread level. Bake for 20 minutes until well risen and the tops spring back when gently pressed with a fingertip.

Allow the cakes to cool in the tins for 5 minutes then loosen the edges and turn out onto a wire rack. Peel off the lining paper and leave to cool completely.

Arrange one of the cakes on a serving plate and spread with the jam. The strawberries, if using, can be added to the jam layer and/or the top. Top with the second cake. Dust with a little extra sugar to decorate. Cut into slices to serve.

Note:
Traditional Victoria sponges, as served in National Trust cafés, are sandwiched with a layer of jam. For an indulgent treat, you can lightly whip 150ml double cream and spoon this over the jam before topping with the second cake.

Simple Buttercream

This is quick to make, and keeps well in the fridge for 2–3 days
or in the freezer for up to 2 months. It can be used instead of
whipped cream in Victoria Sponge Cake.

150g butter, softened
300g icing sugar, sifted
About 1 tablespoon milk
(optional)
Food colouring (optional)

FLAVOURING (CHOOSE ONE)
A few drops of vanilla essence

Finely grated zest and juice of
½ a lemon or ½ an orange
1 teaspoon of instant coffee
dissolved in a teaspoon of
cold water
20g cocoa blended with a little
water to make a smooth paste
75g dark chocolate, melted

Cream the butter until soft and fluffy. Add the icing sugar in two
or three batches, continuing to cream until the mixture is white
and resembles whipped cream.

Beat in your chosen flavouring. If the mixture seems stiff, beat
in a little milk.

If using food colouring, add it drop by drop from the end of
a skewer, mixing between each addition.

French Buttercream

**Lower in sugar than simple buttercream, this is delicious but a little
fiddly. A mixer on a stand, or a hand-held electric whisk, is essential.
A helper and a sugar thermometer are also useful.**

225g unsalted butter,
   at room temperature
120g granulated sugar
60ml water
4 egg yolks
Pinch of salt

FLAVOURING (CHOOSE ONE)
A few drops of vanilla essence
Finely grated zest and juice of
   ½ a lemon or ½ an orange
1 teaspoon of instant coffee
   dissolved in a teaspoon of
   cold water
20g cocoa blended with a little
   water to make a smooth paste
75g dark chocolate, melted

Cut the butter into about 16 chunks.

Put the sugar in a small pan and add the water. Set over low heat
and stir gently from time to time until all crystals have dissolved.

Put the egg yolks in the mixer bowl and beat fast for 4–5 minutes,
until thick and creamy (use a large metal bowl if working with
a hand whisk).

Make sure every sugar crystal has dissolved, then bring the syrup to the boil and boil fast, without stirring, to 115°C or soft ball stage (when a little dropped in cold water forms a soft ball). Take care, the sugar is very hot.

As soon as the sugar reaches temperature, begin whisking the yolks fast and pour the syrup in a thin, steady stream between the beater and the side of the bowl, whisking until all is incorporated.

Add a pinch of salt and your chosen flavouring (unless using cocoa or chocolate, in which case beat in after the butter), then whisk in the butter, one chunk at a time, beating until it is well mixed before adding the next chunk.

This buttercream will keep in the fridge for 2–3 days or can be frozen for up to 2 months. Defrost for a couple of hours before using. Use instead of whipped cream or buttercream – it's especially nice with coffee cakes (see page 68).

Note:
Don't waste those egg whites. You have enough here to make two batches of meringues (page 100). The only other ingredient you need is a little caster sugar. Alternatively, make some financiers (page 88).

Madeira Cake

A perfect cake for afternoon tea on any occasion. It's called Madeira cake because it was considered good with Madeira wine.

200g butter, softened, plus
   a little for greasing
200g caster sugar
4 eggs
Finely grated zest of 1 lemon

200g self-raising flour,
   plus a little for the tin
1–2 tablespoons milk or water
A large thin slice of citron peel

Preheat the oven to 160°C. Line the base of a deep 20cm diameter cake tin with non-stick baking paper or greaseproof paper. Lightly grease the sides and dust with a little flour.

Put the butter and sugar in a large bowl and beat together until pale and fluffy. Add the eggs one by one, beating well between each one. Add a tablespoon of the flour with each egg if the mixture curdles.

Once all the eggs have been added, stir in the lemon zest. Sift in the flour and mix gently but thoroughly. Add a little milk or water to slacken the mixture very slightly.

Put the mixture in the prepared tin and level the top. Place the citron peel on top, roughly in the centre. Bake for 1–1½ hours. Check after an hour. If it seems to be browning too fast turn the oven down to 150°C. The cake is done if the surface springs back when gently pressed with a fingertip.

Leave to cool in the tin for 10–15 minutes, then turn out on to a wire rack and leave to cool completely.

Coffee and Walnut Cake

Another favourite from National Trust tearooms. This cake
is relatively plain and needs a rich icing. French buttercream
(see page 64) is also good with this.

SPONGE CAKE

175g soft margarine
175g caster sugar
3 eggs
175g self-raising flour
½ teaspoon baking powder
2 teaspoons instant coffee
  dissolved in 3 teaspoons
  boiling water
40g walnut halves, chopped

BUTTERCREAM

115g butter, at room
  temperature
225g icing sugar, sifted
3 teaspoons instant coffee
  dissolved in 3 teaspoons
  boiling water
100g ready chopped mixed
  nuts, lightly toasted, cooled
4 walnut halves, cut in half

Preheat the oven to 180°C. Brush two 20cm Victoria sandwich tins with a little oil and line the bases with non-stick baking paper.

Add the margarine and sugar to the bowl of an electric mixer and beat until light and fluffy. Gradually beat in the eggs, little by little and beat well after each addition. If the mixture looks as if it may curdle, beat in a little flour.

Mix the flour with the baking powder then fold into the creamed mixture. Add the dissolved coffee and chopped nuts and fold together. Divide the mixture evenly between the two tins, spread level and bake for about 20 minutes until well risen and the tops spring back when pressed with a fingertip.

Leave the cakes to cool in the tin for 5 minutes then loosen the edges, turn out on to a wire rack and peel off the lining paper. Leave to cool.

To make the buttercream, beat the butter, icing sugar and dissolved coffee together until light and fluffy. Use one quarter of the buttercream to sandwich the cakes together then spread about one third of the remaining icing over the sides of the cake.

Sprinkle the chopped nuts over a sheet of non-stick baking paper then coat the sides of the cake in the nuts by holding the cakes on their side and rolling in the nuts.

Transfer to a cake plate, spread half the remaining buttercream thinly over the top of the cake, mark into 8 portions then spoon the remaining buttercream into a piping bag fitted with a large star tube and pipe a whirl of buttercream on each portion and top with a piece of walnut.

Chocolate Hazelnut Cake

**A rich but light, flourless chocolate cake for special occasions.
It can be made and filled a few hours in advance.**

120g hazelnuts (skin on)
4 tablespoons cocoa
120g dark chocolate
   (70% cocoa solids)
120g butter, softened, plus
   a little for greasing
120g caster sugar
6 eggs, separated
1 tablespoon strong coffee

Pinch of salt
Icing sugar for dusting
Raspberries and extra cream
   (optional), to serve

FOR THE GANACHE

150ml double cream
75g dark chocolate
   (70% cocoa solids), chopped

Preheat the oven to 160°C. Grease 2 x 20cm diameter shallow
tins and line the bases with non-stick baking paper.

Chop the hazelnuts finely or grind to a coarse powder in a food
processor. Mix in the cocoa. Break the chocolate into a bowl and
place over simmering water to melt.

Cream the butter, add the caster sugar and beat until light and pale.
Beat in the egg yolks one by one. Stir in the melted chocolate, add
the coffee and salt and mix well.

Whisk the egg whites until stiff. Add a third of them to the mixture and stir well, then fold in the remainder. Fold in the nut and cocoa mixture. Divide between the tins, shaking to level the mixture. Bake for 20–25 minutes, until the tops are firm to the touch and the cakes are coming away from the sides a little. Cool in the tins for about 10 minutes, then turn out on to a wire rack and leave until cold.

To make the ganache: heat the cream to just below boiling point. Add the chopped chocolate, stirring until it melts. Leave to cool. Whisk until it thickens and becomes a paler brown.

Use the ganache to sandwich the cakes. Dust the top with icing sugar and serve with a few raspberries and some extra cream if liked.

Rhubarb and Ginger Cake

This is developed from a recipe given by Marika Hanbury Tenison in her *Book of Afternoon Tea* (1980). For other rhubarb-based goodies, try visiting Clumber Park in Nottinghamshire, home to the National Collection of Rhubarb. Over 130 varieties are grown there, including 'Early Victoria', Holstein Blut' and 'Grandad's Favourite'.

FOR THE RHUBARB LAYER

30g butter

30g soft brown sugar

About 50g golden syrup

400–500g rhubarb, trimmed weight

FOR THE CAKE

100g butter, softened

100g soft brown sugar

1 egg

200g plain flour

2 teaspoons ground ginger

1 teaspoon bicarbonate of soda

200g black treacle, slightly warmed

75g candied ginger, cut in small dice

2–3 tablespoons milk

Preheat the oven to 160°C. Use non-stick baking paper to line a deep tin with a fixed base, 20cm square or 18–20cm diameter round.

To make the rhubarb layer, melt the butter, sugar and syrup over gentle heat. Pour the mixture into the lined tin, letting it run all over the base. Cut the rhubarb into short lengths and arrange it on top, closely packed together in a single layer.

To make the cake, cream the butter and then beat in the sugar until pale and fluffy. Add the egg and beat again. Sift the flour, ginger and bicarbonate of soda together and stir into the mixture; don't worry if it seems dry. Add the treacle and stir well. Finally add the chopped ginger and slacken the mixture with a little milk. Spoon over the rhubarb, level the top, and bake for 1¼–1½ hours, until the top is firm to the touch.

Leave to cool in the tin for at least 30 minutes, then invert on to a serving plate and peel off the paper. Cut into 8 large or 16 daintier pieces. Serve with cream or crème fraîche.

Lemon Drizzle Cake

With loaf-shaped cakes, there sometimes seems to be too much cake
and not enough drizzle. This makes a shallow cake with lots of
lemony syrup.

100g butter
200g self-raising flour
100g caster sugar
2 large eggs, lightly beaten
100ml milk
Finely grated zest of 1 lemon

FOR THE DRIZZLE TOPPING

Juice of 3 medium lemons
   and finely grated zest
   of 1 lemon
100g granulated sugar
   plus 2 tablespoons

Preheat the oven to 180°C. Line a shallow cake tin, about 18 x 25cm, with non-stick baking paper.

Put the butter in a pan and heat gently until just melted (if substituting margarine, use a soft type and add directly to the mix).

Sift the flour and caster sugar together into a bowl. Add the eggs, milk and lemon zest, then pour in the butter. Use a stick blender to mix all together. Scrape the batter into the lined tin, levelling it and spreading it into the corners.

Bake for 20–25 minutes. Leave to cool slightly in the tin (about 10 minutes) before adding the drizzle.

Pierce the top of the cake all over with a toothpick. Mix the lemon juice and zest with the 100g granulated sugar and spoon it over the still-warm cake, a little at a time, allowing one lot to sink in before adding more. Finally, sprinkle the remaining 2 tablespoons of sugar over the top. Cool completely before slicing: eight large pieces if it is the main event, 12 daintier ones for an elaborate tea.

Fruit Cake

Suitable for Christmas, birthdays and other celebrations.

250g butter, softened, plus a little
    for greasing
250g caster sugar
6 eggs
250g plain flour
2 tablespoons rum, brandy or milk
1 teaspoon baking powder
2 teaspoons mixed spice (optional)
¼ teaspoon salt

1 tablespoon cocoa (optional)
250g currants
250g raisins
250g sultanas
125g glacé cherries, rinsed
    of syrup, dried and halved
125g blanched almonds,
    chopped coarsely
125g candied peel, chopped

Preheat the oven to 150°C. Grease and line a deep 20cm diameter cake tin using a band of non-stick baking paper that projects a few centimetres above the top of the tin.

Cream the butter and sugar together in a large bowl. Beat in the eggs one by one, adding a tablespoon of flour after each of the last three to help prevent the mixture curdling. Stir in the rum, brandy or milk.

Sift the baking powder, spice, salt, cocoa, if using, and the remaining flour together. Put the currants, raisins, sultanas and cherries into a bowl and stir in a few tablespoons of the flour mixture. Then stir half the remaining flour mixture into the egg mixture. Add the fruit, almonds and peel and mix again. Finally, add the remaining flour mixture and stir lightly but thoroughly.

Put the mixture in the prepared tin, smooth the top and hollow it slightly in the centre. Bake in the middle of the oven for 3–4 hours, or until a skewer inserted in the centre of the cake comes out clean.

Leave the cake in the tin until completely cold, then remove and peel off the paper. Store in a tin for at least 3 weeks before use.

Drizzle a tablespoon of rum or brandy over the base every few days if liked. Decorate with almond paste and royal icing, or serve plain with Wensleydale cheese, as preferred.

Sunday and Christmas Teas

Sunday tea punctuated a day that was often unimaginably tedious, when no shops were open and children were seen and not heard, especially in church. Country children might at least have a chance to be outside, but those in towns often spent a dull day on their best behaviour. Meals, sometimes with friends or relations as guests, could be light relief or an ordeal, depending on the family.

> **Meals, sometimes with friends or relations as guests, could be light relief or an ordeal, depending on the family.**

The Sunday tea tradition of proletarian post-war Britain included two or three foods regarded as huge treats. One was ham, which has a long connection with special teas, mentioned by both Charlotte Brontë and Charles Dickens in their novels. The others, tinned salmon followed by tinned peaches (often eaten with evaporated milk), are the products of industrial food preservation. Nowadays these might be regarded as quaintly retro, but are not, perhaps, to current taste.

For those who consume a Sunday roast earlier in the day, food needs to be light. A nicely made ham salad (page 48) is still appreciated, as are plain ham sandwiches or maybe sausage rolls (page 104). Potted fish (pages 43 and 44) with bread and butter or toast are good alternatives. Add salad and a cheeseboard for variety. A light cake such as a whisked sponge (page 58) with cream and

berries in summer or
lemon curd (page 148)
in winter makes the meal more
special; or offer a lemon drizzle cake (page 74) or a choice of smaller
items such as madeleines (page 86) and coffee kisses (page 92).

Christmas Day might seem an occasion when no one has room
for tea except to drink, but Christmas teas have their own rituals.
Bread, butter and jam fade into the background, but elegant little
nibbles such as smoked salmon pinwheels might be welcome
(page 26), or perhaps some smoked trout pâté (page 43). A piece
of blue Stilton and some celery (proper, blanched white celery)
always appeared on our family Christmas tea table, along with nuts,
little oranges and candied fruit. Large stand pies and trifles graced
the tables of relatives and friends, and there was always a Christmas
cake (fruit cake, page 76), either iced or served with cheese, according
to family and local traditions.

Parkin

Parkin is solid food for hungry people. Look for it in local tearooms and bakeries after a bracing walk in Upper Wharfedale or around Malham Tarn in North Yorkshire.

100g butter
3 tablespoons golden syrup
100g granulated sugar
150g plain flour
150g medium oatmeal

2 generous teaspoons
    ground ginger
1 teaspoon bicarbonate
    of soda
150ml milk

Preheat the oven to 130°C. Line a deep 20cm square tin with non-stick baking paper (if the tin has a loose base, fold the paper to fit but don't make cuts in it).

Put the butter and syrup in a saucepan and melt over gentle heat.

Put all the dry ingredients in a bowl and mix together well. Pour in the syrup and butter mixture. Add the milk and stir well to make a very sloppy mixture.

Pour into the lined tin and bake for about 1¼ hours, until the parkin is set and firm to the touch. Don't open the oven door during the first hour, or it will fall.

Leave to cool in the tin, then remove and wrap in foil or store in a tin for 2–3 hours before cutting.

Fruit Loaf

Fruit loaves, filling and sustaining, are associated with farmhouse food of the type found in hilly areas, such as the Lake District's Borrowdale valley.

450g dried fruit (sultanas, raisins, currants, chopped candied peel)
300ml strong tea (hot or cold), such as Assam
170g soft light brown sugar

350g self-raising flour
1 large egg, beaten
30g butter, melted
A little mixed spice
Butter, to serve

Put the dried fruit in a large bowl, pour the tea over the fruit and leave to soak overnight or for 6–8 hours.

Preheat the oven to 170°C. Grease a 900g loaf tin and line with non-stick baking paper.

Add all the remaining ingredients to the fruit and tea and mix well. Spoon into the prepared tin and bake for 1¼–1½ hours, until firm to the touch. Leave to cool in the tin.

Slice and serve well buttered.

Bara Brith

Bara brith (the Welsh term for 'speckled bread') can be
made with baking powder, but it's nicest raised with yeast.

200ml milk
100g soft brown sugar
30g fresh yeast
500g strong plain flour
½ teaspoon salt
1 teaspoon mixed spice

100g butter, cut in cubes,
  plus extra to serve
150g raisins
150g currants
60g mixed candied peel, chopped
1 egg, beaten

Warm the milk until hand-hot, add a pinch of the sugar and crumble
in the yeast. After a few minutes it should froth, showing that the
yeast is working.

Mix the flour with the remaining sugar, salt and spice and rub in the
butter. Add the fruit and peel. Stir in the yeast mixture and the egg to
make a dough (add a little more milk if necessary). Knead well, then
place in a large bowl, cover with clingfilm and leave in a warm place
until doubled in size (about 1–1½ hours).

Grease a 900g loaf tin. Knock back the dough and shape into a loaf. Place in the tin and leave to prove for 30–45 minutes.

Preheat the oven to 190°C. Bake the loaf for 1 hour, covering the top with foil after the first 30 minutes. Check if it is done by tapping the underside: the loaf should sound hollow. If not, bake for up to 30 minutes longer, checking from time to time.

Leave to cool on a wire rack. Serve thinly sliced and buttered.

Note:
Fresh yeast can be bought from the bakery department in many supermarkets. I find it much more reliable than dried yeast, which comes in confusing variety and tends to get tired within a few weeks of the tin being opened.

Small Cakes
and Biscuits

Madeleines

The mixture for these little cakes can be prepared well in advance.

100g butter, plus 2 tablespoons,
   melted, for the tins
100g plain flour, plus
   1 tablespoon for the tins
1 teaspoon baking powder

Pinch of salt (optional)
2 eggs
100g caster sugar
2 teaspoons orange
   flower water

You will need two madeleine trays (with shell-shaped hollows) or bun trays: mix 2 tablespoons melted butter with 1 tablespoon flour, and prepare the trays by brushing the hollows with this mix.

In a small pan, melt the 100g butter until it foams, turns light brown and smells deliciously nutty. Pour into a bowl and leave to cool but not solidify.

Sift the 100g flour with the baking powder; if using unsalted butter add a pinch of salt.

Whisk the eggs and sugar together until pale and thick. Stir in the sifted flour mix, then pour in the cooled melted butter and orange flower water. Stir gently until all is incorporated. Cover and chill, along with the prepared trays, for at least an hour or overnight.

To bake, preheat the oven to 180°C. Half fill each little hollow in the prepared trays; the mixture will be stiff, but it spreads during baking. Bake for 8 minutes, then check: the cakes should be firm and may have developed the characteristic humped shape (but don't worry if they remain flat). Allow another 1–2 minutes baking if necessary.

Remove from the oven, leave for a moment, then remove from the trays and cool on a wire rack. Madeleines are nicest eaten within an hour of baking, but will keep for a couple of days in an airtight tin.

Financiers

Traditionally baked in small oblong moulds, gilded from the heat, these were thought to resemble gold bars, hence the name. Ordinary muffin moulds produce a less distinctive shape, but work just as well.

80g ground almonds
30g self-raising flour, sifted, plus a little for dusting
120g icing sugar, sifted
Pinch of salt

3 egg whites
120g butter, plus a little for greasing
2 tablespoons flaked almonds, to decorate

Mix the ground almonds, flour, icing sugar and salt. Add the egg whites and stir briefly, just enough to make a batter.

Melt the butter in a saucepan over medium heat and heat it until it foams, turns a slightly darker gold and gives off a nutty smell. Strain it through a sieve lined with kitchen paper or muslin, discarding any residues. Stir the butter into the almond mixture, combining thoroughly. Chill for about 2 hours.

Grease a 12-hole muffin tray and dust lightly with flour; put the tray in the fridge.

To bake, preheat the oven to 180°C. Put the batter in a jug or piping bag and divide it among the muffin moulds. Scatter a few flaked almonds over the top of each one to decorate.

Bake for 10–12 minutes. Cool in the tray for a few minutes and then turn out onto a wire rack. Delicious with rose-petal tea, or Oolong.

Brownies

Another National Trust tearoom favourite, this quick gluten-free recipe uses ingredients from the store cupboard.

175g soft margarine
65g cocoa
300g caster sugar
3 eggs, beaten

1 ½ teaspoons vanilla extract
Pinch of salt
115g gluten-free,
    self-raising flour

Preheat the oven to 180°C. Line a 20cm shallow square cake tin with a large square of non-stick baking paper, snipping the paper diagonally into the corners of the tin and pressing the paper down so that the base and sides of the tin are lined.

Heat the margarine in a medium-sized saucepan over a low heat, stirring until just melted. Mix in the cocoa and stir until dissolved. Take the pan off the heat and stir in the sugar. Lightly beat the eggs, vanilla and salt together. Beat half the egg mixture into the cocoa then beat in the remaining mixture until smooth. Mix in the gluten-free flour and beat until smooth.

Pour the brownie mixture into the lined tin, spread into an even layer then bake for 18–20 minutes or until well risen, lightly cracked around the edges and the centre has a slight wobble.

Leave to cool in the tin for 15 minutes then mark into 10 bars and leave to cool completely. Lift the brownies out of the tin holding the paper then cut into bars and peel off the paper.

Mrs Jenks' Petticoat Tails

Mrs Jenks was the cook at Kingston Lacy, Dorset, during the Bankes family era. This is her recipe for shortbread. The method makes tiny, bite-sized biscuits, just right for an elegant but light tea.

250g butter, softened
125g caster sugar

350g plain flour
125g ground rice

Preheat the oven to 160°C. Cream the butter and sugar together. Mix in the flour and ground rice, and knead lightly to make an even-textured dough.

Divide into 15 pieces (50g each) and roll each into a ball. Press each one out on a baking tray to make a disc about 8cm in diameter, leaving space for them to spread slightly. Neaten the edges, prick all over with a fork, and cut each disc into six pieces. Bake for 20–25 minutes until a very pale gold colour. Cool for a few minutes, then place on a wire rack to cool completely.

Coffee Kisses

The Be-Ro Book, first published in 1923 by the Be-Ro flour company, was a standby in ordinary twentieth-century kitchens such as those at the Hardmans' House in Liverpool, or Mr Straw's House in Worksop, Nottinghamshire. This recipe is adapted from it.

175g self-raising flour,
 plus a little for dusting
75g soft brown sugar
75g butter, cut into cubes,
 plus a little for greasing
2 teaspoons instant coffee
 dissolved in 1 tablespoon
 hot water

1 egg, lightly beaten
Chocolate-coated coffee beans
 or chocolate drops (optional)
Simple buttercream (page 62)
 or French buttercream
 (page 64) flavoured with
 coffee, or chocolate ganache
 (page 70)

Preheat the oven to 180°C. Grease two baking trays.

Mix the flour and sugar, and rub in the butter. Stir in the coffee and egg to make a soft dough. Divide this into 40, keeping the portions as equal as possible.

On a lightly floured surface, roll each piece into a ball and flatten slightly. Place on the baking trays, bearing in mind they will roughly double in size. If desired, decorate half of them by pressing a chocolate-coated coffee bean or a chocolate drop in the middle.

Bake for about 15 minutes, until well risen and firm to touch. Cool on a wire rack. Shortly before needed, sandwich one plain and one decorated biscuit with buttercream or ganache.

Note:
Chocolate coffee beans look and taste good but add an unexpected crunch: leave them out if you think this won't be popular.

Macarons

Macarons need precision, so allow time for making them. Orange and chocolate are the suggested flavours here in honour of Terry's, creators of the Chocolate Orange and former owners of Goddards in York, a National Trust house built in the 1920s.

100g icing sugar
100g ground almonds
70g egg white
Small pinch of salt
50g caster sugar
A few drops of orange flavouring

A few drops of orange
  food colouring
Chocolate ganache (page 70)
  or buttercream (page 62)
  flavoured with cocoa

You will need a silicone macaron mat with a baking tray underneath, or two baking trays lined with non-stick baking paper.

Put the icing sugar and almonds in a food processor and whizz together. Tip into a sieve over a bowl and rub as much of the mixture through as possible.

Put the egg white and salt in a large bowl and use an electric mixer to whisk to soft peaks. Add the caster sugar and keep whisking until the mixture is glossy and stiff (about 2 minutes on high speed). Add the orange flavouring and colouring followed by the almond and icing sugar mixture. Stir until the mixture flows in a ribbon off the spoon and disappears back into the mixture in 10–20 seconds.

Put the mixture in a piping bag with a plain round 1cm nozzle. Pipe a test of about 1 teaspoonful mixture: it should flow into a neat round (if it doesn't, stir a little more). Pipe about 30 small even rounds until all the mix is used. Tap the tray sharply to remove air and then leave for about an hour, until the tops are no longer sticky to the touch.

Preheat the oven to 140°C. Bake the macarons for 12–15 minutes, until firm on top. Leave the macarons to cool for about 20 minutes, then remove to a wire rack to cool completely. Sandwich with ganache or buttercream. Eat soon after making.

Lemon Biscuits

'Delicious', said Miss M.L. Allen of her recipe for Sugar Cakes, the original lemon biscuit, in *Five O'Clock Tea* (1887). She was absolutely right.

250g flour, plus a little for dusting
125g butter, cut into cubes, plus a
   little for greasing
Pinch of salt

125g caster sugar, plus
   a little for dusting
Finely grated zest of 1 lemon
1 large egg, beaten

Sift the flour into a bowl and rub the butter into the flour. Stir in the salt, sugar and lemon zest, then mix to a stiff dough with the egg.

Dust a work surface with a little flour and roll the dough into a rope about 3–6cm in diameter, depending on whether you want tiny biscuits or larger ones. Wrap tightly in foil and chill well. (The dough can be frozen at this stage if desired; defrost for a couple of hours in the fridge before use.)

When ready to bake, preheat the oven to 130°C. Grease two or three baking trays.

Unwrap the dough and cut crossways into 5mm thick slices. Put a little caster sugar on a plate and dip the upper surface of each slice in it before placing, plain side down, on a baking tray.

Bake for 25–30 minutes until crisp. The biscuits should remain pale. Cool on a wire rack. Best eaten the day they are baked.

Grantham Gingerbread

**Light, crunchy ginger biscuits, associated with a town that
was once an important stop on the route north from London.**

120g butter, softened
250g caster sugar
1 large egg, separated
250g flour, plus a little for dusting

2 generous teaspoons
  ground ginger
1 teaspoon baking powder
Pinch of salt

Preheat the oven to 130°C. You will need several baking trays,
either non-stick, or lined with non-stick baking paper.

Cream the butter and sugar together until light and fluffy, then stir
in the egg yolk. Mix the flour, ginger, baking powder and salt and
sift into the butter mixture. Whisk the egg white. Add to the other
ingredients and press together to form a firm dough. Knead for a
minute to make sure it is even.

Dust a work surface with flour. Cut the dough into four equal pieces
and roll each one into a rope about 2cm in diameter. Cut each rope
into eight and roll each piece into a ball. Place on the baking trays,
allowing space for the mixture to spread during baking.

Bake for 30–40 minutes until the biscuits are pale fawn and firm
to the touch. Leave on a wire rack to cool completely and store in
an airtight tin.

Brandy Snaps

Brandy snaps are simple to make and delicious to eat. Honey is not essential but a little mixed with the syrup gives a lovely flavour.

30g golden syrup
20g runny honey (or use 50g syrup and omit the honey)
50g butter
50g soft light brown sugar
1 teaspoon lemon juice
2 teaspoons brandy (or omit this and replace with lemon juice)
50g plain flour

Pinch of ground ginger
A little finely grated lemon zest

TO SERVE
150ml double cream, whipped, or clotted cream
2 balls of stem ginger in syrup, drained and sliced thinly (optional)

Preheat the oven to 170°C. Grease two baking trays.

In a small pan, melt together the syrup, honey if using, butter and sugar. Stir in the lemon juice and brandy, if using.

Put the flour, ginger and lemon zest in a bowl, then pour in the syrup and butter mixture and stir to make a runny batter.

Drop generous teaspoonfuls 8–10cm apart on the greased trays and bake for 7–10 minutes. They will spread and form lacy biscuits.

When nicely coloured, remove from the oven, leave to cool for a minute or two, then use a spatula to lift them off the tray and quickly roll each one around the handle of a wooden spoon. Slide off and cool on a wire rack. Best eaten the day they are made, but can be stored for a few days in an airtight container.

To serve, add a spoonful of cream to both ends of each brandy snap. If you like, decorate the cream with a slice of preserved ginger.

Meringues

Crisp white meringues with cream are a treat any time. Add flavours to suit the season.

2 egg whites
115g caster sugar

SEASONAL OPTIONS
2 tablespoons lemon curd
    (page 148), which you can make
    with your 2 egg yolks and a few
    chopped blanched pistachios
Whipped cream
2 tablespoons elderflower cordial
    and a selection of summer berries

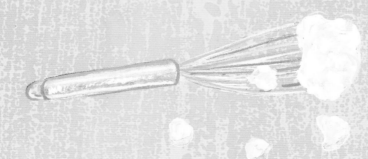

To make the meringues, preheat the oven to 110°C and line a large baking sheet with non-stick baking paper. Whisk the egg whites in a large, dry grease-free bowl until thick enough to stand in moist-looking peaks. If you can turn the bowl upside down without the whites moving, they are ready.

Gradually whisk in the sugar a teaspoonful at a time until all the sugar has been added. Continue to whisk for a minute or two more until the meringue is very thick and glossy.

Spoon onto the lined trays to make eight small round meringues. Hollow the tops slightly. Bake for 1–1¼hours or until the meringues may be lifted easily off the paper and the centre is still slightly soft. Leave to cool.

Note:
To serve in winter, fill the hollows with lemon curd and whipped cream marbled together and scatter a few chopped pistachios over the top. In summer, flavour the whipped cream with elderflower cordial. Divide it among the meringues and arrange a few berries on top.

Meringues freeze well (without fillings) so don't worry about making more than you need.

Pastries

Sausage Rolls

Quickly made using bought pastry and good-quality sausages – squeeze the sausage meat out of the skins. The meat can be used as it is, or seasoned as below.

Flour for dusting
1 pack (300–350g) ready-rolled
   puff pastry
500–600g sausage meat or sausages
   with the skins removed
Beaten egg, cream or milk
   for glazing

<u>SEASONING (OPTIONAL)</u>
2 cloves of garlic, roughly chopped
50ml water
2 teaspoons chilli flakes
2 heaped teaspoons smoked
   paprika
4 teaspoons sweet paprika

Preheat the oven to 200°C.

For the seasoning, if using, put the garlic and water in a blender and whizz to make a paste. Add it to the sausage meat together with the chilli flakes, smoked and sweet paprika and stir well.

Dust a work surface lightly with flour and unroll the pastry on it. Using a rolling pin, roll lightly to make it a little thinner. Cut the pastry in half lengthways.

Take half the sausage mixture and shape it into a long roll; place along one side of the pastry. Repeat with the remaining pastry and sausage. Carefully fold the pastry over the sausage, sealing the edges with water. Brush over the top with beaten egg, cream or milk. Cut each roll into 2cm long pieces: you should have 10–12 from each.

Place on a baking tray and bake for 20–25 minutes until well risen and golden brown. Best eaten when just cool.

Sausage Rolls with Glamorgan Sausage

Glamorgan sausage is a mixture of cheese, leeks and breadcrumbs, bound with egg. It makes a good vegetarian alternative to ordinary sausage filling.

3 large leeks, trimmed, washed and thinly sliced

250g Caerphilly cheese (Lancashire or feta are good alternatives)

100g freshly made white breadcrumbs

1 generous teaspoon made English mustard

A little finely grated lemon zest

Salt and black pepper

1 egg, beaten, plus a little extra for glazing (or use cream or milk)

Flour for dusting

1 pack (300–350g) ready-rolled puff pastry

Preheat the oven to 200°C.

Put the sliced leek in a bowl and pour boiling water over it. Leave for 30 seconds, then tip into a sieve, run cold water through it and drain thoroughly. Put it in a bowl and crumble in the cheese. Add the breadcrumbs, mustard and lemon zest, and mix lightly. Taste the mixture and add salt, pepper and a little more mustard if desired. Stir in the beaten egg.

Dust a work surface with flour and unroll the pastry on it. Using a rolling pin, roll lightly to make it a little thinner. Cut the pastry in half lengthways.

Take half the leek mixture and shape it into a long roll; place along one side of the pastry. Repeat with the remaining pastry and leek mixture. Carefully fold the pastry over the filling, sealing the edges with water. Wash over the top with beaten egg, cream or milk. Cut each roll into 2cm long pieces: you should have 10–12 from each.

Place on a baking tray and bake for 20–25 minutes until well risen and golden brown. Best eaten when just cool.

Savoury Profiteroles

Choux pastry is not difficult to make and these little profiteroles
work well with various fillings: try smoked salmon chopped in little
pieces and mixed with dill and cream cheese; chicken and curried
mayonnaise (page 29); or chicken liver pâté (page 52), mixed with
a little cream to slacken it. The profiteroles can be frozen uncooked,
then baked direct from the freezer, as can gougères (page 110) and
éclairs (page 114).

75g strong plain flour
50g butter, cut into cubes
125ml water

Pinch of salt
2 eggs, beaten
Filling of your choice (see above)

Preheat the oven to 220°C. You will need two baking trays,
either non-stick or lined with non-stick baking paper.

Choux paste:
Sift the flour on to a plate or a piece of paper. Put the butter, water
and salt into a pan and heat. Once the butter has melted and the
mixture is at a rolling boil, remove it from the heat and shoot all the
flour in at once. Stir well with a wooden spoon until the mixture has
formed a stiff batter and leaves the sides of the pan. Continue to stir
over low heat for about 3 minutes. Remove from the heat and leave
to cool slightly.

Add the eggs gradually, beating until the mixture is smooth, even
and holds its shape (you may not need to add all the beaten egg).

Profiteroles:
Use 2 teaspoons to shape this choux paste into blobs on the baking trays, or pipe through a plain 1cm nozzle.

Bake for 10 minutes, then reduce the heat to 180°C and continue cooking until the profiteroles are crisp at the sides as well as on top.

Remove to a wire rack. Make a slit in the side of each profiterole to allow steam to escape and leave to cool completely.

When cool, spoon or pipe in your chosen filling, and garnish with sprigs of herbs to complement the filling.

Little Cheese and Bacon Gougères

A gougère is cheese-flavoured choux pastry; it is generally baked in one large ring, but the mix can be shaped into little buns.

4 rashers of very thinly sliced
  bacon or pancetta
40g Cheddar or other strongly
  flavoured cheese, grated

½ teaspoon made English
  mustard (optional)
1 quantity choux paste
  (page 108)

Preheat the oven to 220°C. You will need two baking trays, either non-stick or lined with non-stick baking paper.

Cook the bacon until very crisp. Drain it well and crumble it into small pieces.

Mix the cheese and mustard into the choux paste, stirring well. Then stir in the bacon. Use 2 teaspoons to shape the paste into blobs on the baking trays.

Bake for 10 minutes, then reduce the heat to 180°C and continue cooking until the gougères are crisp at the sides as well as on top.

Remove to a wire rack. Make a slit in the side of each to allow steam to escape. Serve warm or just cooled.

Little Salmon and Watercress Quiches

Little quiches for afternoon tea need to be really small but this can mean a high ratio of pastry to filling. Try shaping in muffin tins, or patty pans of the type used for jam tarts (which make smaller quiches).

Flour for dusting
About 200g shortcrust pastry,
    home-made or bought
300g hot-smoked salmon, flaked
About 50g watercress, large
    stems removed

3 tablespoons chopped fresh dill
5 eggs
250ml crème fraîche
100ml milk
1 scant teaspoon salt
Black pepper

Preheat the oven to 200°C and place a couple of baking trays in to heat up.

Dust a work surface with flour. Roll the pastry out thin and cut rounds to fit the chosen moulds. Line the moulds with pastry and distribute the flaked salmon among them.

Chop the watercress and dill together and scatter some over the top of each quiche.

Beat the eggs, crème fraîche, milk, salt and pepper together. Put the mixture in a jug and pour a little into each quiche. Don't over-fill, or the mixture will spill out as it cooks.

Place the moulds on the hot trays and bake for 15–20 minutes depending on size. Leave to cool a little in the moulds, then remove to a wire rack. Best served just cooled.

Leek and Gruyère Tartlets

Leek and Gruyère cheese is a lovely combination. For afternoon tea these tartlets should be very small: try muffin tins or patty pans of the type used for jam tarts to contain the pastry.

25g butter
2–3 leeks, trimmed (remove the
  greenest part of the leaves),
  washed and finely chopped
Flour for dusting
About 200g shortcrust pastry,
  home-made or bought

100g Gruyère cheese,
  finely grated
300ml single cream
3 eggs
1 teaspoon French mustard
About ½ teaspoon salt
Black pepper

Preheat the oven to 200°C and place a couple of baking trays in to heat up.

Melt the butter in a frying pan and cook the leeks very gently (don't let them brown). When tender, transfer to a bowl and leave to cool.

Dust a work surface with flour. Roll the pastry out thin and cut rounds to fit the chosen moulds.

Put a little of the cooled cooked leek in each pastry case. Top with some of the grated cheese. Beat the cream, eggs, mustard, salt and pepper together. Put the mixture in a jug and distribute among the tarts, being careful not to over-fill.

Place the moulds on the hot trays and bake for 15–20 minutes depending on size. Leave to cool a little in the moulds, then remove to a wire rack. Best served just cooled.

Note:
If you want to make one large tart, use the pastry to line a 23cm diameter tart tin. Line the pastry with greaseproof paper and cover this with baking beans. Cook for 15 minutes, then remove the beans and paper, add the leeks, the cheese and the egg mixture, and return to the oven for about 30 minutes, until the centre is just set.

Chocolate Éclairs

Always a delicious choice for afternoon tea.

1 quantity choux paste (page 108)
About 300ml whipping cream

FOR THE CHOCOLATE ICING
150g caster sugar
100ml water
35g butter
75g dark chocolate (60–70%
    cocoa solids), chopped

Preheat the oven to 220°C. You will need two baking trays, either non-stick or lined with non-stick baking paper.

Spoon the choux paste into a piping bag fitted with a plain 1cm nozzle. Pipe 5–6cm lengths on to the prepared trays.

Bake for 10 minutes, then reduce the heat to 180°C. Continue cooking until they are crisp at the sides as well as on top.

Remove to a wire rack. Slit each éclair along the side and scoop out any soft dough with a teaspoon handle, then leave to cool. The éclairs can be prepared a few hours ahead up to this point.

To make the chocolate icing, put the sugar and water in a small pan. Stir gently over low heat until every sugar crystal has dissolved. Make sure none are left on the sides of the pan. Bring to the boil and turn off the heat. Leave to cool for a few minutes, then stir in the butter and the chocolate. Stir occasionally as it cools for about 10 minutes.

Whip the cream. Pipe or spoon some into each éclair. Quickly dip the top of each éclair in the icing. Chill well until set. Eat on the day of making.

Maids of Honour

Maids of honour are a rich variety of curd tart, associated with Richmond, London. The origin of the curious name is unknown.

40g butter, softened
40g caster sugar
1 egg yolk
About 120g curd cheese
40g ground almonds
Finely grated zest of ½ a lemon

Pinch of ground cinnamon
3 tablespoons rum
  or brandy
Flour for dusting
1 pack (300–400g) ready-rolled
  puff pastry

Preheat the oven to 200°C and put two baking sheets in to heat.

Beat the butter and sugar together, then stir in the egg yolk. Mash the curd cheese well to remove lumps, then add it to the butter mix, along with the almonds, lemon zest, cinnamon and rum or brandy, and stir thoroughly.

Dust a work surface with flour. Spread the pastry out and roll gently to make it a little thinner. Use a plain 8cm diameter cutter to cut out as many rounds as possible, then carefully stack the trimmings, press together, re-roll and cut again. Use the discs of pastry to line two bun tins. Stir the filling again gently and carefully add a generous teaspoon to each tart.

Put the tins on the heated baking sheets and bake for 15–20 minutes, by which time the pastry should be well risen and the filling patched with gold-brown. Cool on a wire rack and eat within about 3 hours of baking.

Note:
The filling can be prepared the day before and kept in the fridge.

Nursery and Birthday Teas

Nursery teas and schoolroom teas belong to a seemingly distant age, yet it is less than a century since children in big houses had their own nurses and maids, and governesses or tutors to give them basic education, and apartments such as the nursery and schoolroom at Lanhydrock in Cornwall.

Children were considered to need plain food: a simple tea of boiled eggs, bread and butter and something uncomplicated such as shortbread. Cakes were thought over-rich and pernicious to their health. Pizza was unheard of, but mashed sardines seem to have been popular for sandwiches. One pleasure children did have was making toast in front of an open fire, rescuing the bread, dusty and slightly smoked from the ashes, when it fell off the toasting fork.

> Children were considered to need plain food ... Cakes were thought over-rich and pernicious to their health.

When sent away to school, boys were given a 'tuck box' which always seemed to include a fruit cake (page 76). Florence White, in *Good Things in England* (1932), included a vignette of cricket tea at Knightshayes in Devon, the boys piling clotted cream on plum cake or trickling golden syrup over bread and clotted cream. Poor children were more likely to be given a doorstep of bread with dripping or cheap jam, though many children in the mid-twentieth century began their cooking careers with drop scones (page 130).

Birthday teas for children were occasions when the rules were relaxed. Well into the 1970s, they principally featured sweet food. Victoria sponge (page 60) often appeared, baked as one large cake or as small cakes, iced and decorated with hundreds and thousands, glacé cherries or silver dragées. In the 1950s and 60s the mixture was made into butterfly cakes with buttercream (page 62). Other treats included little bread rolls spread with egg mayonnaise (page 28, but often made with salad cream), plus jelly and custard or, best of all, ice cream. Naturally, there was a birthday cake with candles, which was often a fruit cake. Food was taken at a dining table, and the drink was tea, in cups and saucers, perhaps with orange squash as an alternative. Contemporary tastes probably run more to sausage rolls (page 104) and smoked salmon pinwheels (page 26).

Of course, birthday teas are not confined to children, but adults have autonomy in their daily choices. However, a flourless chocolate cake (page 70) might be appreciated by anyone as a treat on a special day.

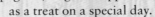

Raspberry Linz Biscuits

Crumbly little biscuits which look a little like old-fashioned raspberry buns but are made with Linzertorte dough, based on hazelnuts.

75g hazelnuts, skinned
180g plain flour
120g butter, cut into cubes,
    plus a little for greasing
Generous pinch of ground
    cinnamon

50g icing sugar
Pinch of salt
Finely grated zest of 1 lemon
1 egg, beaten
2–3 tablespoons good-quality
    raspberry jam

Preheat the oven to 180°C. Grease two baking trays.

Put the hazelnuts in a food processor and whizz until they are reduced to powder. Add the flour, butter, cinnamon, icing sugar, salt, lemon zest and about two-thirds of the egg. Process again to mix.

Turn the mixture out on to a work surface and press together with your fingers. If it seems very dry, add a little more egg. Divide into 24 equal pieces and roll into balls. Flatten each one a little, place on the baking tray and make an indent on the top with your thumb. Place a small blob (about ¼ teaspoon) of jam in each.

Bake for 15–20 minutes, until the little biscuits are light brown and firm. Cool on a wire rack.

Bakewell Tart

Easy to make, a good teatime treat.

About 300g ready-made
  shortcrust pastry
2–3 tablespoons good-quality
  raspberry jam
160g butter, softened
160g caster sugar

2 eggs
A few drops of almond essence
160g ground almonds
50g plain flour, plus a little for
  dusting
2 tablespoons flaked almonds

Preheat the oven to 200°C and put a baking tray in to heat up. For the tart, you will need a shallow oblong tin, 25–30cm x 15–18cm, about 3cm deep.

Dust a work surface with a little flour and roll out the pastry into an oblong slightly bigger than the tin. Line the tin with it, easing well into the corners, trimming as necessary and neatening the edges. Spread the jam over the base.

Cream the butter and sugar together, then beat in the eggs. Stir in the almond essence, followed by the ground almonds and finally the flour. Drop spoonfuls of the mixture over the jam, then use a fork to smooth the filling into an even layer, completely covering the jam. Scatter the flaked almonds over the top.

Bake for 20–25 minutes until golden brown and firm to the touch. Cool in the tin. Cut three by six to give 18 blocks, or as desired.

Freshly Baked

Fruit Scones

National Trust tearooms around the country are proud of their scones. Serve simply with good strawberry jam and generous spoonfuls of clotted cream for the perfect afternoon tea.

450g self-raising flour, plus
  extra for dusting
115g soft margarine, plus
  extra for greasing

85g caster sugar
85g sultanas
1 egg, beaten
200ml milk

Preheat the oven to 200°C. Add the flour and margarine to the bowl of an electric mixer and run in the margarine until the mixture resembles fine crumbs. Stir in the sugar and sultanas.

Add the egg and gradually mix in 150ml of the milk to make a soft dough. Knead lightly on a floured surface then roll out thickly to a generous 2cm thickness, or two fingers. Stamp out circles using a 7cm fluted biscuit cutter and transfer the scones to a lightly greased baking sheet. Knead the trimmings and continue rolling and stamping until you have made 8 scones.

Brush the top of the scones with a little of the remaining milk then bake for 10–15 minutes until well risen and golden brown. Serve warm, split and topped with clotted cream and jam.

Cheese and Marmite Scones

Little savoury scones; the controversial ingredient is subtle, so you don't have to be a Marmite lover to enjoy these.

250g plain flour, plus
   a little for dusting
1 heaped teaspoon baking powder
50g butter, cut into cubes

75g mature cheddar,
   finely grated
150ml milk
1 tablespoon Marmite

Preheat the oven to 200°C. Dust a baking tray with flour.

Sift the flour and baking powder into a bowl. Rub in the butter until the mixture resembles fine breadcrumbs, then stir in the cheese. Beat the milk and Marmite together until blended, then add all but about a dessertspoon of this to the flour mixture. Stir together well to make a soft dough.

Dust a work surface with flour and roll or pat out the dough to a rectangle roughly 2cm thick. Cut out rounds with a 2cm diameter cutter, pressing the scraps together to cut more. Brush over the tops with the remaining milk and Marmite mixture.

Bake for about 15 minutes. Serve warm or just cooled, with butter if liked.

Potato Scones

Tattie scones, boxty, potato cakes – Scotland, Ireland, and north-western England (especially Lancashire) make good use of potatoes for comforting teatime food.

About 500g floury potatoes, peeled
2 teaspoons salt
50g butter, plus extra for cooking
  and serving
About 100g plain flour, plus
  a little for dusting

OPTIONAL ADDITIONS
Chopped chives
3–4 rashers of bacon, fried
  until crisp and then crumbled
4–6 spring onions,
  finely sliced

Steam the potatoes until tender, mash them with the salt and butter, then leave until cool enough to handle.

Start to mix in the flour gradually: you are aiming for a dough that will hold together but is not crumbly. Not all the flour may be needed. This is also the time to add any of the optional ingredients, stirring them in well.

Turn the mixture on to a floured surface and divide into four equal pieces. Pat each portion out to a circle about 1cm thick, making sure it doesn't stick to the surface. Cut each into quarters – farls – or cut with a heart-shaped cutter if you're feeling frivolous.

Heat the griddle or a heavy frying pan and add a little butter. When it foams, put in the scones to cook gently. Leave for 4–5 minutes; golden-brown spots should have formed underneath. Flip each piece to cook on the other side. Remove to a warm plate and cook the remaining scones in the same way.

Serve warm with extra butter and strong Indian tea, or maybe a cup of Lapsang Souchong.

Buckwheat Blinis
with Smoked Salmon

Yeast-raised blinis made with buckwheat flour are well worth the effort. They are best eaten fresh. Serve off a board, as they tend to stick to plates.

150ml milk
15g fresh yeast (see note
   on page 83)
75g plain yoghurt
1 egg, separated
100g strong plain flour
100g buckwheat flour
1 scant teaspoon salt

TO SERVE
About 100g crème fraîche
200g smoked salmon, thinly sliced
Fresh herbs such as dill, tarragon
   or chervil

Heat the milk until it's just hand-hot. Put it in a small bowl and add the yeast. After a few minutes the mixture should froth. Stir in the yoghurt and the egg yolk.

Put the flour, buckwheat flour and salt in a large bowl. Add the yeast mixture and stir to make a batter. Cover the bowl with clingfilm and then leave in a warm place for about an hour, by which time the batter should be bubbly.

Beat the egg white until stiff and fold this into the batter. Cover and leave for another 1–2 hours.

To cook, heat a griddle or a heavy frying pan, preferably non-stick, over moderate heat (if it isn't non-stick, lightly butter the pan between batches). Stir the batter and drop generous teaspoonfuls on to the hot surface. They will spread a little. When holes appear in the top, flip the blinis to brown the other side. Remove to a dish and repeat until the batter is used up.

These are best served when just cooled. Top each one with a little crème fraîche and a generous ribbon of smoked salmon and garnish with a tiny sprig of herbs.

Drop Scones

Also known as Scotch pancakes, these are simple to make and nice
for children to try. The challenge lies in getting the scones equal in
size, nicely round, and golden brown on both sides.

125g self-raising flour
½ teaspoon salt
1 tablespoon sugar
1 large egg, lightly beaten

150ml milk
1 tablespoon melted butter,
  plus extra to serve

Put the flour, salt and sugar in a bowl and mix in the egg to make
a paste. Stir in the milk, little by little, to make a smooth batter (or
whizz all these ingredients together in a food processor or blender).
Add the melted butter.

Heat a griddle or a heavy frying pan, preferably non-stick, over medium heat for 3–4 minutes. If it isn't non-stick, grease it lightly. Make a test scone by dropping a tablespoon of the mixture on to the heated surface (for a good round shape, pour the mixture off the end of the spoon). After a minute or two, when little holes begin to form on the top of the scone, flip it to cook the other side for 2–3 minutes. If the batter seems a bit thick, slacken with a tablespoon or two of extra milk or water. Once you are happy with the texture, cook the remaining batter, keeping the cooked scones warm on a plate in a low oven.

Serve hot with butter. They are also good with cinnamon sugar (page 38), clotted cream, honey and bananas (page 31), or fromage frais, fresh berries and a little sugar.

Parmesan and Chive Drop Scones

A lovely savoury alternative to traditional drop scones.

125g self-raising flour
½ teaspoon salt
1 large egg, lightly beaten
150ml milk
1 tablespoon melted butter,
   plus a little for greasing

2 tablespoons finely grated
   Parmesan
1 generous tablespoon
   chopped chives
Butter, to serve

Put the flour and salt in a bowl and mix in the egg to make a paste.
Stir in the milk, little by little, to make a smooth batter (or whizz all
these ingredients together in a food processor or blender). Add the
melted butter, Parmesan and chopped chives. Cook as directed for
ordinary drop scones (page 130).

Serve hot with butter.

Welsh Cakes

Little cakes, baked on a *planc* (a griddle or girdle), often made for tea in many parts of Wales. Visit Llanerchaeron, a National Trust house in Ceredigion, on the right day and you may taste samples freshly baked on the Edwardian range in the kitchen there.

500g plain flour, plus a little
   for dusting
1 teaspoon baking powder
Pinch of salt
200g butter and lard mixed,
   cut into cubes
200g caster sugar
½ teaspoon mixed spice

100g currants
2 eggs, beaten
A little milk (optional)

TO SERVE
Caster sugar, cinnamon sugar
   (page 38), butter or honey

Mix the flour, baking powder and salt in a large bowl. Rub in the lard and butter and stir in the sugar, spice and currants. Add the eggs and mix to give a dough with the consistency of shortcrust pastry (add a tablespoon or two of milk if it seems very dry).

Dust a work surface with flour and roll out the dough to about 1cm thick or slightly less. Use a 5cm diameter cutter to cut out rounds.

Heat a lightly greased griddle or a heavy frying pan over very gentle heat. Bake the cakes on the griddle for about 3 minutes on each side. The inside must be cooked through.

Eat warm from the griddle, dusted with sugar or served with butter or honey.

Regional Teas

Different parts of the British Isles have their own notions of teatime goodies, based on local traditions of baking. The best known is a 'cream tea' of scones (page 124), jam and clotted cream. This has its origins in the food traditions of Devon and Cornwall, where sometimes the scones were replaced by small rich bread rolls known as splits or chudleighs.

Cornish teas might also include saffron cake or buns (page 140). These are just one example of the large number of regional cakes made in the British Isles, sometimes yeast leavened. They include Sally Lunns (page 139), particularly associated with Bath; Welsh cakes (page 133) and bara brith (page 82), both still popular in Wales; and potato scones (page 126), a feature of teas in Lancashire, parts of Scotland and (as boxty) in Ireland.

> Yorkshire is renowned for lavish teas and tea cakes - flat round bread buns with currants, served warm ... and often dripping with melted butter.

Yorkshire is another county renowned for lavish teas and tea cakes (page 138) – flat round bread buns with currants, served warm or reheated by toasting, and often dripping with melted butter – were a special treat on cold winter days. Gingerbreads and biscuits also have many regional variations. Oatmeal parkin (page 80) was a speciality of Yorkshire and the Pennine spine of northern England, but numerous other places had ginger-spiced sweet things: the biscuits associated with Grantham in Lincolnshire (page 97) are one example. Variations on curd tarts are found in Yorkshire, Lincolnshire and the north Midlands, and also in the south, as Richmond's maids of honour (page 116).

The seaside has its own tradition of teas, often including shellfish of various kinds, from boiled winkles or cockles with bread and butter, to crab sandwiches in smart cafés. Best of all were shrimp teas. These could be simple – bread and butter and a measure of boiled brown shrimps, to be leisurely (and messily) shelled by the consumer. Potted shrimps are more elegant; they can be purchased as shrimps in spiced butter (look out for these in the Formby area; they are a speciality of the Lancashire and south Lakes coast), or can be home-made (page 44).

Muffins

These are proper English muffins, of the sort sold freshly baked in the streets of late nineteenth-century London. Keeping the dough warm is the key to making them well.

500g strong plain flour
2 teaspoons salt
450ml milk and water mixed
½ teaspoon sugar
30g fresh yeast (see note
  on page 83)

30g butter, lard or olive oil,
  plus a little for greasing
Rice flour or semolina for dusting
Butter to serve

Put the flour in a large bowl and scatter the salt round the edge. Leave in a warm place (an airing cupboard, or an oven with residual heat) for 10–20 minutes.

Put the milk, water and sugar in a pan and warm until hand-hot. Crumble in the yeast and leave until frothy. Melt the butter or lard, if using.

Add the yeast mixture and fat to the flour and mix well for
5 minutes to make a very soft dough (it is too soft to knead).
Cover the bowl with clingfilm and return it to the warmth for
1–1½ hours, until the dough is well risen.

Dust a work surface and a tray with rice flour or semolina. Turn
the dough on to the surface and cut into 10 or 12 pieces. Shape into
rounds, place on the dusted tray, cover with a clean dry tea towel
and leave to prove for about 30 minutes.

Heat a griddle or a large heavy frying pan and grease it lightly.
Cook the muffins for about 4 minutes on each side until golden
brown in patches. Keep warm until all are done.

They are best eaten while still warm. Make a shallow incision around
each one, then pull apart into two pieces. Put a thin slice of butter on
the cut sides. If the muffins have gone cold, split them and toast the
inside, then add butter and jam.

Teacakes

Soft bread buns with a little fruit, good for tea in winter.

250ml milk
30g fresh yeast (see note
  on page 83)
500g strong plain flour,
  plus a little for dusting

Pinch of salt
60g sugar
60g butter, cut into cubes,
  plus a little for greasing
80g sultanas

Put the milk in a pan and warm until hand-hot. Crumble in
the yeast and leave for a few minutes until frothy.

Mix the flour, salt and sugar in a bowl and rub in the butter. Stir
in the yeast mixture and knead to a smooth dough. Cover with
clingfilm and leave to rise for about an hour.

When doubled in size, knock back and knead in the sultanas. Divide
into six pieces. Dust a work surface with flour and roll each piece of
dough into a ball, then roll out to give a disc about 1.5cm thick. Put
the cakes on two large greased baking trays, cover with a clean dry
tea towel and leave to prove for about 30 minutes.

Preheat the oven to 220°C. Bake the teacakes for 15–20 minutes
until golden brown.

Remove from the oven, rub the top of the hot cakes with buttered
kitchen paper, then cover with a clean tea towel and leave to cool. Eat
fresh, sliced and buttered, or next day, split, toasted and buttered.

Sally Lunn

There are many legends about how this brioche-like bun got its name.
It is said to come from the bakery of Sally Lunn, now one of the oldest
houses in Bath, Somerset. It is a good item for tea after walking the
Bath Skyline or admiring the Palladian Bridge at nearby Prior Park.

Butter for greasing
Pinch of sugar
75ml hand-hot water
15g fresh yeast (see note
  on page 83)
125ml single cream

1 whole egg and 1 egg yolk
Finely grated zest of
  ½ a lemon
250g strong plain flour,
  plus a little for dusting
½ teaspoon salt

Lightly grease a deep cake tin, about 15cm diameter.

Add the sugar to the water, crumble in the yeast and stir gently to
mix. When it froths, beat in the cream, egg, egg yolk and lemon zest.

Put the flour in a large bowl and add the salt. Pour in the yeast
mixture and stir for 5 minutes until everything is well combined.
Scrape the dough on to a floured surface and form into a round. Put
this in the buttered tin, cover with a clean dry tea towel and leave in
a warm place to rise for 1–1½ hours.

Preheat the oven to 200°C. Bake the bun for 15 minutes; if it seems a
bit pale, turn the oven down to 170°C and give it an extra 5 minutes.

Eat warm. Tear or cut the bun into two or three layers, spread
liberally with clotted cream or butter, and put it back together again.

Saffron Buns

Saffron gives a gentle pale gold colour to these traditional Cornish buns. Allow plenty of time to make them, and be sure to keep the dough warm.

Generous pinch of saffron
150ml hand-hot water
15g fresh yeast (see note on page 83)
40g caster sugar
250g strong plain flour, plus a little for dusting

½ teaspoon salt
80g butter, softened and cut into flakes
60g currants
30g candied lemon peel, chopped
2 tablespoons sugar and 1 tablespoon milk to glaze

Toast the saffron in a small pan for a couple of minutes. Crumble into a bowl with a tablespoon of warm water. Leave for at least 30 minutes, or overnight.

Mix the warm water, yeast and a pinch of sugar and leave until frothy. Put the flour in a bowl, sprinkle the salt round the edge and half the sugar in the middle. Pour in the yeast mixture, cover with flour from the sides and leave until the yeast froths. Add the saffron and butter. Mix to a soft dough and knead for a few minutes. Cover the bowl with clingfilm and leave in a warm place for 3–4 hours.

Dust a work surface with flour and grease two baking trays. Knock back the dough and knead in the remaining sugar, the currants and peel. Divide into eight equal pieces and shape into balls on the floured surface. Place on the baking trays, cover lightly with clingfilm and leave to prove in a warm place for 2–3 hours. They will not rise much.

Preheat the oven to 210°C. Bake the buns for about 15 minutes.

To glaze, dissolve the sugar in the milk in a small pan, then bring to the boil and bubble for a moment. Brush over the buns while still hot from the oven.

Eat the same day, with clotted cream or butter if you like.

Belvoir Castle Buns (1869)

Florence White, who recorded this recipe in *Good Things in England* (1932) wrote: 'These buns were made at Belvoir Castle and were greatly liked by the Duke of Rutland, who often asked for them.' Belvoir Castle in Leicestershire is where afternoon tea is thought to have originated in about 1840.

flour, plain, 2lb. (900g)
butter, 5 oz. (140g)
sugar, 6 oz. (170g)

yeast, 1 oz. (30g)
milk, 1 pint (570ml)
currants, 6 oz. (170g)

Place the flour in a basin. Add the butter and rub it in until the mixture looks like breadcrumbs. Mix in the sugar.

Place the yeast in a small basin and cream it with a little sugar. Take 1 gill (140ml) of the milk, let it boil and add to the remainder of the milk. Add this to the yeast and pour it into the centre of the flour. Stir in the flour from the sides.

Cover the basin with a clean towel, set it in a warm place and let it rise for 2 hours.

Knead it and divide it into 6 pieces. Roll out the dough very thinly and over each piece sprinkle some of the currants.

Fold each piece up and cut into strips, and turn them upside down on a buttered and floured tin. Let them rise for 30 minutes and bake for 10 minutes.

Preserves and Drinks

Strawberry Jam

National Trust properties include many lovely kitchen gardens and
orchards, whose produce went into sweet preserves. Strawberries
were always popular. Home-made strawberry jam may not set like
'shop' jam but it has a delicious freshness. Perfect for scones, toast,
for sandwiching Victoria sponge cakes, or just with bread and butter.

1.5kg small, ripe strawberries
800g jam sugar (sugar with
    added pectin)

500g granulated sugar
Juice of 2 lemons

Put a saucer in the freezer or fridge and sterilise several jars.

Hull the strawberries and clean them if necessary (wiping with damp
kitchen paper is the best way). Crush about half of them lightly. Put
all the fruit in a large thick-bottomed pan with the sugars and lemon
juice. Warm over low heat, stirring all the time until the sugar has
completely dissolved, then bring to the boil.

Boil rapidly for about 15 minutes. Towards the end of this time, check
for set by putting a drop of jam on the cold saucer and returning it to
the fridge or freezer for a moment: if it wrinkles when pushed with a
finger, the jam is ready.

Remove from the heat, skim off any froth, and leave to settle for a
few minutes. Pot into warmed sterilised jars. Put a waxed disc on
the surface of the jam and seal with a lid. Label when the jam is
completely cold. Store in a cool place.

Pear and Ginger Jam

Some National Trust estates, such as Croome in Worcestershire, include many species of apple and pear trees. Use under-ripe cooking pears for this jam, a gentle, warming combination for hot toast or toasted muffins on chilly winter days.

500g pears (weighed
   after peeling and coring)
1 large cooking apple,
   peeled and cored
100ml water

Finely grated zest and juice
   of 1 lemon
500g granulated sugar
2–3 pieces of stem ginger in syrup,
   drained and cut in small slices

Put a saucer in the freezer or fridge and sterilise your jars.

Cut the pears in thin slices and chop the apple. Put the fruit in a thick-bottomed pan with the water, lemon zest and juice and simmer gently until the pears are translucent and the apple is soft.

Add the sugar and stir to dissolve. Add the ginger and bring to the boil. Cook over moderate heat, stirring from time to time for about 15 minutes; it will need more constant stirring as it nears setting point as it tends to stick: be careful, as it is thick and can spit. Check for set by putting a drop of jam on the cold saucer: if it forms a skin and wrinkles when pushed with a finger, the jam is ready.

Pot into warmed sterilised jars. Put a waxed disc on the surface of the jam and seal with a lid. Label when the jam is completely cold. Store in a cool place.

Lemon Curd

Use to sandwich cakes or macarons, on toast or muffins, or in little sandwiches. Lemon curd is a good way of using leftover egg yolks.

60g unsalted butter
Finely grated zest and juice
   of 1–2 lemons

2 egg yolks
80–100g caster sugar (depending
   on how sweet you'd like it to be)

Put the butter in a small saucepan and heat until it just melts. Stir in all the other ingredients and cook over moderate heat, whisking all the time, for about 10 minutes, or until the mixture has thickened to the texture of custard and a spoon drawn across the base of the pan leaves a trail. Be careful not to over-heat or the egg will curdle.

Pot into a sterilised jar, cover and label. Store in the fridge or a cool pantry. Eat within a month.

Blackberry Jelly

Collecting blackberries and making jelly is one of the pleasures of late summer. The pectin content of blackberries is adequate but not high, so I use half granulated sugar and half jam sugar (with added pectin) to get a pleasing soft-set jelly.

1kg blackberries
Sugar (see method)

Put the blackberries in a large pan and add water to just cover. Bring to the boil and simmer, stirring occasionally, for about 20 minutes, or until the fruit is soft and has released all the juice. Tip the contents of the pan into a jelly bag set over a large bowl and leave the juice to drip through overnight.

Next day, put a saucer in the freezer or fridge and sterilise several jars.

Measure the juice; for each litre of juice, weigh 750g sugar. Warm the sugar in a low oven. Put the juice in a thick-bottomed pan and heat until it is not far from boiling. Then add the sugar and stir well. When the sugar has completely dissolved, bring to the boil and boil rapidly for about 10 minutes to setting point. Check for set by putting a drop of jelly on the cold saucer: if it forms a skin and wrinkles when pushed with a finger, the jelly is ready.

Pot immediately into warmed sterilised jars. Put a waxed disc on the surface of the jelly and seal with a lid. Label when the jelly is completely cold. Store in a cool place.

Crab Apple Jelly

Orchards like those at Killerton in Devon or Brockhampton in Herefordshire, provided apples for cider, puddings and preserves, such as this lovely, perfumed, deep red jelly.

About 1.5kg crab apples, weighed after removing any debris
About 1.5kg granulated sugar (see method)

A handful of rose geranium leaves, washed and tied in a bunch

Wash the apples, chop roughly and put in a thick-bottomed pan. Add water to just cover, and stew gently, stirring from time to time, until reduced to a mush. Tip the contents of the pan into a jelly bag set over a large bowl and leave the juice to drip through overnight. Next day, put a saucer in the freezer or fridge and sterilise several jars.

Measure the juice; for every 500ml juice, weigh 500g sugar. Put the juice and sugar into the cleaned pan and stir over gentle heat until the sugar has completely dissolved. Add the bunch of geranium leaves.

Boil rapidly to setting point. The mixture should deepen in colour to a beautiful dark red. After about 10 minutes, test for set by putting a drop of jelly on the cold saucer: if it forms a skin and wrinkles when pushed with a finger, the jelly is ready.

Remove the geranium leaves, leave to settle for a moment and then pot into warmed sterilised jars. Put a waxed disc on the surface of the jelly and seal with a lid. Label when the jelly is completely cold. Store in a cool place.

The Regent's, or George the Fourth's, Punch

We are amateurs at tea punches when compared to some from the past. This recipe was recorded by Eliza Acton in *Modern Cookery for Private Families* (1845). Should you feel inclined to try this, a modern version of the recipe noted that it is 'absolutely lethal', so treat it with respect.

'*Pare as thin as possible the rinds of two China oranges, of two lemons, and of one Seville orange, and infuse them for an hour in half a pint of thin cold syrup; then add to them the juice of the fruit. Make a pint of strong green tea, sweeten it well with fine sugar, and when it is quite cold, add it to the fruit and syrup, with a glass of the best old Jamaica rum, a glass of brandy, one of arrack, one of pine-apple syrup and two bottles of champagne; pass the whole through a fine lawn sieve until it is perfectly clear, then bottle, and put on ice until dinner is served. We are indebted for this receipt to a person who made the punch daily for the prince's table, at Carlton Palace, for six months, and it has been in our possession for some years and may be relied on.*'

Champagne Cocktail

A glass of something sparkling lifts afternoon tea from a little treat to something more akin to the lavish hospitality once associated with houses such as Cliveden in Berkshire. To make things doubly festive make a classic champagne cocktail.

1 sugar cube
2 dashes angostura bitters
20ml cognac
Champagne to fill up the glass

TO DECORATE (OPTIONAL)
Lemon juice
Caster sugar

Prepare decorated glasses in advance: pour a little lemon juice into a saucer and put a layer of caster sugar in another. Carefully dip the outer edge of the rim into the juice and rotate to give a line about 5mm deep all the way round. Then dip into the caster sugar and rotate to frost the rim. This can be done several hours in advance.

For each cocktail, put a sugar cube in a teaspoon and add the bitters. Drop it into a glass and pour over the cognac. Top up with the champagne.

Kir Royale

Usually served as an aperitif, kir is simply a mix of white wine with crème de cassis, a blackcurrant liqueur produced in Burgundy. Kir royale uses champagne or sparkling wine. Crème de framboise (raspberry liqueur) is sometimes used instead of crème de cassis.

Put a generous teaspoon of crème de cassis or blackcurrant liqueur into each glass. Add champagne or other sparkling wine to fill up the glass.

Note:
A small bottle of crème de cassis and two bottles of sparkling wine will make kir for 10 people.

Earl Grey Tea and Gin Cocktail

A refreshing tea-based cocktail for a hot day, with a mildly bitter note. Most preparation can be done in advance.

200g sugar
200ml water
2 teaspoons Earl Grey tea, or 2
  good-quality Earl Grey tea bags
160ml gin

3–4 strips of zest from
  an unwaxed orange
1 ripe peach, preferably white
Crushed ice
Soda water

First, make a sugar syrup: put the sugar and water in a small saucepan and heat, stirring constantly to dissolve the sugar. When every crystal is dissolved, bring to the boil, then remove from the heat. Cool. This will make more than you need, but the syrup can be stored in a jar in the fridge for a week or two.

Put the tea in a small jug, pour over the gin and add the orange zest. Leave to infuse for 2 hours, then strain, discarding the tea and orange zest. Peel the peach by pouring boiling water over it and slipping off the skin.

When ready to serve, half fill 4 tall glasses with crushed ice. Divide the gin among them, then add 40ml of sugar syrup to each one. Top up with chilled soda water. Slice the peach thinly and add 3–4 slices to each glass, along with a straw or a stirrer.

Pimm's Cup

Pimm's No. 1 Cup is a gin-based drink, normally topped up with fizzy lemonade and some fruit and mint leaves; careful additions make all the difference to a good Pimm's.

200ml Pimm's No. 1 Cup
A few long strips of
   lemon zest
½ an orange, thinly sliced
A length of cucumber about
   4cm long, cut in thin slices

6–8 long sprigs of mint (reserve
   the 4 nicest for garnishing)
Ice cubes
600ml fizzy lemonade, ginger ale
   or tonic water
A few strawberries, sliced

Mix the base about an hour before needed. Put the Pimm's in a small jug or bowl. Gently bruise the lemon zest to release the oils, add to the Pimm's, along with the orange slices, and stir. Add the cucumber. Take the leaves of 2–4 of the mint sprigs and crush the leaves a little to release the scent. Stir into the mix. Chill.

When needed, take a pretty serving jug and fill about two-thirds with ice cubes. Pour in the Pimm's mixture. Top up with the lemonade or other mixer.

Serve in tall glasses, making sure each glass gets a fair share of ice cubes and additions. Garnish each one with a sprig of mint and a few slices of strawberry.

Funeral Teas

Funeral teas serve several purposes. On a practical level, they provide sustenance for those attending, some of whom may have travelled a long way. They are also an opportunity to express sympathy to the nearest and dearest of the deceased and, unless the circumstances of the death are extremely distressing, to reminisce affectionately.

Reminiscences can be more private, of course. When Benjamin Disraeli, her friend and former prime minister died in 1881, Queen Victoria travelled to his residence at Hughenden in the Chiltern Hills, Buckinghamshire. After viewing the coffin she took tea in the library of the house where they had talked two years previously.

Forecasting numbers for a funeral tea is difficult. This unpredictability makes the organiser's task far from easy, even if a caterer or hotel is providing the meal. Over-catering is the only real answer to the possibility of running short of food.

> To be 'buried with ham' was considered the height of respectability in the late nineteenth and early twentieth centuries.

Although funeral teas are based on the general plan of formal afternoon teas, one should veer towards the less frivolous side of things, and more substantial portions. For anyone faced with organising such an event independently, a good option is sandwiches of ham (to be 'buried with ham' was considered the height of respectability in the late nineteenth and early twentieth centuries), beef, cheese and alternative fillings (pages 22–23), along with some savoury pastries (pages 104–113). A good fruit cake (page 76), some scones (page 124), or slices of buttered fruit loaf (page 81) are always welcome. The tastes of the deceased may be taken into account as a form of remembrance.

A glass of something – sherry, or stronger – invariably goes down well on these occasions (unless, of course, the deceased or family are teetotallers, in which case, stick to tea, preferably of the strong Indian variety). It helps to warm those who have stood at a chilly graveside, bolsters the emotions and breaks down formality. It may seem odd, but some of the best tea parties are those held after funerals.

Index

Acknowledgements

Thanks to friends and family who have helped test and taste recipes and discussed their favourite tea ideas with me: the Mummery family, Claire Monteith and Steve Huckfield, Michele Webster, Carole Hick and Jan Alice Merry. Helen Saberi generously shared her knowledge of all things tea-related and gave me access to the draft of her forthcoming book, *Teatimes: past and present*. Felicity Cloake's column *'How to Make the Perfect...'* (theguardian.com) was invaluable for helping me pick my way through the forest of information about several recipes.

Finally, my thanks go to all at the National Trust and Pavilion who have worked on this book, especially Peter Taylor, Kristy Richardson and Maggie Ramsey.